EXEGETICAL
GEMS FROM
# BIBLICAL
# GREEK

# EXEGETICAL GEMS FROM BIBLICAL GREEK

## A REFRESHING GUIDE
### to Grammar and Interpretation

## BENJAMIN L. MERKLE

**B**
**Baker Academic**
*a division of Baker Publishing Group*
Grand Rapids, Michigan

© 2019 by Benjamin L. Merkle

Published by Baker Academic
a division of Baker Publishing Group
PO Box 6287, Grand Rapids, MI 49516-6287
www.bakeracademic.com

Printed in the United States of America

Library of Congress Cataloging-in-Publication Data
Names: Merkle, Benjamin L., 1971– author.
Title: Exegetical gems from biblical Greek : a refreshing guide to grammar and interpretation / Benjamin L. Merkle.
Description: Grand Rapids : Baker Academic, a division of Baker Publishing Group, 2019. | Includes bibliographical references and index.
Identifiers: LCCN 2018053550 | ISBN 9780801098772 (pbk.)
Subjects: LCSH: Bible. New Testament. Greek. | Bible. New Testament—Criticism, interpretation, etc. | Greek language, Biblical—Grammar. | Bible. New Testament—Language, style.
Classification: LCC BS1938 .M47 2019 | DDC 225.4/87—dc23
LC record available at https://lccn.loc.gov/2018053550

ISBN 978-1-5409-6211-9 (casebound)

Baker Publishing Group publications use paper produced from sustainable forestry practices and post-consumer waste whenever possible.

# CONTENTS

CONTENTS

# INTRODUCTION

## Why This Book?

In one sentence, I wrote this book as a tool to help current and former students of New Testament Greek prosper and ultimately succeed in using the Greek they worked so hard to acquire. Because there is currently no book like this one, allow me to explain its uniqueness. The 2017 book that I coauthored with Robert Plummer offered practical strategies for acquiring Greek, maintaining it, and getting it back if it becomes rusty.[1] That book is intended to encourage and inspire without getting too deep into the details of Greek grammar and syntax. It also offers some powerful testimonies from pastors who use their Greek in ministry, and it presents a few devotional reflections from the Greek New Testament.

In one sense the present book has the same ultimate goal as *Greek for Life*, but it pursues it very differently. As the title indicates, this book offers a collection of "exegetical gems," loosely defined as substantial insights from NT passages gained by a proper knowledge and use of Greek. Knowledge of NT Greek does not answer every exegetical or theological question that people raise. It does, however, make a significant difference in many key passages, providing exegetical answers to debated texts. Seeing such examples is encouraging to current and former students of NT Greek and provides motivation for continued use of the language.

There is another practical outcome of reading this book. Let's face it, reviewing Greek can be difficult and tedious. Even if you have

---

1. Benjamin L. Merkle and Robert L. Plummer, *Greek for Life: Strategies for Learning, Retaining, and Reviving New Testament Greek*, with a foreword by William D. Mounce (Grand Rapids: Baker Academic, 2017).

already taken Greek, reading through an 800-page grammar can be daunting and even discouraging. But what if there were a way to review the basics of Greek syntax without needing to reread a reference grammar? What if there were a tool that not only reviewed such syntax but also demonstrated the exegetical payoff along the way? What if the content of a massive grammar were condensed into less than 200 pages, with dozens of exegetical gems uncovered in the process? That is precisely what this book seeks to accomplish.

### What Is This Book?

This book consists of thirty-five chapters, each of which offers two main things: (1) an exegetical gem from the NT and (2) a review of some aspect of Greek syntax. By the time you finish reading through this book, you will have reviewed all of the basics typically covered in a second-year (or second-semester) Greek syntax and exegesis course. The order in which topics are presented generally follows that of a book I coauthored with Andreas Köstenberger and Robert Plummer.[2]

Each chapter follows the same basic format: (1) introduction, (2) overview, and (3) interpretation. The introduction presents the biblical text containing the exegetical gem for the chapter. It also raises a question that can be answered with a sufficient knowledge of Greek, especially knowledge of the topic covered in the chapter. Then the overview offers a brief account of the relevant aspect of Greek syntax and, within the broader topic, helps situate the precise insight needed to answer the exegetical question. The final, interpretation section applies the newly acquired insight to the exegetical question and offers a solution.

### For Whom Is This Book?

This book can be used in various contexts by a variety of readers, but I will highlight the most obvious audiences:

2. Andreas J. Köstenberger, Benjamin L. Merkle, and Robert L. Plummer, *Going Deeper with New Testament Greek: An Intermediate Study of the Grammar and Syntax of the New Testament* (Nashville: B&H, 2016). Hereafter cited as KMP.

1. *College or seminary students.* This book will be helpful whether you are first learning Greek or are in a more advanced course. For example, if you are currently taking Greek syntax, this book provides numerous examples of how knowing Greek makes a difference in the way we interpret the Bible. Reading this book alongside your main textbook will provide a condensed summary of the material in an accessible format.

2. *Former Greek students.* If you took Greek many moons ago and are a bit rusty, or if you are looking for helpful tools so you don't get rusty, then this book is for you. Although some of you might enjoy casually reading a book on Greek grammar or syntax, most won't find that very appealing. Most grammars are designed as reference tools rather than as classroom textbooks.[3] This book offers you a way to glean new insights from knowing Greek *but at the same time* enables you to review all the basics of Greek syntax.

3. *Greek teachers.* If you teach Greek, you know how difficult it can be to keep students motivated to press on with the hard work of acquiring the language. Students need encouragement along the way, and the best way to motivate them is to show them how knowing Greek makes a difference in understanding and interpreting the Bible. This book gives you thirty-five examples you can use to instruct and inspire your students.

## Who Helped with This Book?

I should mention several people who in some way contributed to this book. First, I thank my good friend Chip Hardy, who was integral in coming up with the concept of this book. Indeed, Chip is the author of *Exegetical Gems from Biblical Hebrew*, the companion volume to this book, also published by Baker Academic. Second, thanks are due to Baker editor Bryan Dyer, who offered valuable feedback along the way and has been a great encouragement to me from the beginning of this project. Third, I am grateful for Alysha Clark, Alex Carr, and David Moss—students at Southeastern Baptist Theological

3. Our *Going Deeper* (KMP) is a notable exception.

Seminary—who helped edit drafts of the manuscript. Fourth, I am thankful for my colleagues at Southeastern who continually challenge me to pursue a deeper love for Christ. Fifth, I am grateful for my supportive wife and my loving children. Finally, I give thanks to my Savior, Jesus Christ, because I once was lost but now am found.

δι᾽ ὑμᾶς ἐπτώχευσεν πλούσιος ὤν, ἵνα ὑμεῖς τῇ ἐκείνου πτωχείᾳ πλουτήσητε.

Though he was rich, yet for your sake he became poor, so that you by his poverty might become rich. (2 Cor. 8:9)

# ABBREVIATIONS

## Frequently Cited Grammars

BDF           F. Blass, A. Debrunner, and Robert W. Funk, *A Greek Gram-
              mar of the New Testament and Other Early Christian Litera-
              ture* (Chicago: University of Chicago Press, 1961)

B&W           James A. Brooks and Carlton L. Winbery, *Syntax of New Tes-
              tament Greek* (Washington, DC: University Press of America,
              1979)

D&M           H. E. Dana and Julius R. Mantey, *A Manual Grammar of the
              Greek New Testament* (Toronto: Macmillan, 1927)

KMP           Andreas J. Köstenberger, Benjamin L. Merkle, and Robert L.
              Plummer, *Going Deeper in New Testament Greek* (Nashville:
              B&H, 2016)

M&E           David L. Mathewson and Elodie Ballantine Emig, *Intermediate
              Greek Grammar: Syntax for Students of the New Testament*
              (Grand Rapids: Baker Academic, 2016)

Porter,       Stanley E. Porter, *Idioms of the Greek New Testament*, 2nd ed.
*Idioms*      (Sheffield: Sheffield Academic, 1994)

Robertson     A. T. Robertson, *A Grammar of the Greek New Testament in
              the Light of Historical Research*, 4th ed. (Nashville: Broad-
              man, 1934)

Wallace       Daniel B. Wallace, *Greek Grammar beyond the Basics: An Ex-
              egetical Syntax of the New Testament* (Grand Rapids: Zonder-
              van, 1996)

Young         Richard A. Young, *Intermediate New Testament Greek: A
              Linguistic and Exegetical Approach* (Nashville: Broadman &
              Holman, 1994)

Zerwick,      Maximilian Zerwick, *Biblical Greek: Illustrated by Examples*,
*Bib. Gk.*    Eng. ed. adapted from the 4th Latin ed. by Joseph Smith
              (Rome: Scripta Pontificii Instituti Biblici, 1963)

## General and Bibliographic

| | |
|---|---|
| × | times |
| AB | Anchor Bible |
| aor. | aorist |
| BBR | *Bulletin for Biblical Research* |
| BDAG | Walter Bauer, Frederick W. Danker, William F. Arndt, and F. Wilbur Gingrich, *A Greek-English Lexicon of the New Testament and Other Early Christian Literature*, 3rd ed. (Chicago: University of Chicago Press, 2000) |
| BECNT | Baker Exegetical Commentary on the New Testament |
| BNTC | Black's New Testament Commentaries |
| BSac | *Bibliotheca Sacra* |
| BTCP | Biblical Theology for Christian Proclamation |
| ca. | *circa*, about |
| CBQ | *Catholic Biblical Quarterly* |
| CEB | Common English Bible |
| cent. | century, centuries |
| chap(s). | chapter(s) |
| CSB | Christian Standard Bible |
| ed. | edition, edited by |
| e.g. | *exempli gratia*, for example |
| EGGNT | Exegetical Guide to the Greek New Testament |
| Eng. | English verse numbering |
| esp. | especially |
| ESV | English Standard Version |
| exp. | expanded |
| fut. | future |
| GTJ | *Grace Theological Journal* |
| HCSB | Holman Christian Standard Bible |
| ICC | International Critical Commentary |
| i.e. | *id est*, that is |
| impf. | imperfect |
| ind. | indicative |
| inf. | infinitive |
| ISV | International Standard Version |
| IVPNTCS | IVP New Testament Commentary Series |
| JBL | *Journal of Biblical Literature* |
| JETS | *Journal of the Evangelical Theological Society* |
| JSNTSup | Journal for the Study of the New Testament Supplement Series |
| KJV | King James Version |

| | |
|---|---|
| L&N | Johannes P. Louw and Eugene A. Nida, *Greek-English Lexicon of the New Testament Based on Semantic Domains*, 2 vols. (New York: United Bible Societies, 1988) |
| LNTS | Library of New Testament Studies |
| LXX | Septuagint |
| NA[28] | *Novum Testamentum Graece*, ed. Eberhard Nestle, Erwin Nestle, B. Aland, K. Aland, J. Karavidopoulos, C. M. Martini, and B. M. Metzger, 28th rev. ed. (Stuttgart: Deutsche Bibelgesellschaft, 2012) |
| NABRE | New American Bible (Revised Edition) |
| NAC | New American Commentary |
| NASB | New American Standard Bible |
| NEB | New English Bible |
| NET | New English Translation |
| NETS | *A New English Translation of the Septuagint*, ed. Albert Pietersma and Benjamin G. Wright, rev. ed. (New York: Oxford University Press, 2014), http://ccat.sas.upenn.edu/nets/edition/ |
| NICNT | New International Commentary on the New Testament |
| NIDNTTE | *New International Dictionary of New Testament Theology and Exegesis*, ed. Moisés Silva, 2nd ed., 5 vols. (Grand Rapids: Zondervan, 2014) |
| NIGTC | New International Greek Testament Commentary |
| NIV | New International Version (2011 ed.) |
| NIV 1984 | New International Version (1984 ed.) |
| NIVAC | NIV Application Commentary |
| NJB | New Jerusalem Bible |
| NKJV | New King James Version |
| NLT | New Living Translation |
| NLV | New Life Version |
| NPNF[1] | *A Select Library of Nicene and Post-Nicene Fathers of the Christian Church*, ed. Philip Schaff, 1st series, 14 vols. (New York: Christian Literature, 1886–90; repr., Grand Rapids: Eerdmans, 1956) |
| NRSV | New Revised Standard Version |
| NT | New Testament |
| opt. | optative |
| OT | Old Testament |
| Phillips | *The New Testament in Modern English*, J. B. Phillips |
| p(p). | page(s) |
| pl. | plural |
| plupf. | pluperfect |
| PNTC | Pillar New Testament Commentary |

| | |
|---|---|
| pres. | present |
| ptc. | participle |
| repr. | reprinted |
| rev. | revised |
| *RevExp* | *Review and Expositor* |
| RSV | Revised Standard Version |
| SBG | Studies in Biblical Greek |
| *SBJT* | *The Southern Baptist Journal of Theology* |
| SBLGNT | *The Greek New Testament: SBL Edition*, ed. Michael W. Holmes (Atlanta: Society of Biblical Literature, 2010) |
| *STR* | *Southeastern Theological Review* |
| subj. | subjunctive |
| TNTC | Tyndale New Testament Commentaries |
| trans. | translated by |
| *TynBul* | *Tyndale Bulletin* |
| Tyndale | William Tyndale's translations (first printed 1525–36) |
| UBS⁵ | *The Greek New Testament*, ed. B. Aland, K. Aland, J. Karavidopoulos, C. M. Martini, and B. M. Metzger, 5th rev. ed. (Stuttgart: Deutsche Bibelgesellschaft, 2014) |
| vol(s). | volume(s) |
| WBC | Word Biblical Commentary |
| ZECNT | Zondervan Exegetical Commentary on the New Testament |

## Old Testament

| | | | | |
|---|---|---|---|---|
| Gen. | Genesis | | Esther | Esther |
| Exod. | Exodus | | Job | Job |
| Lev. | Leviticus | | Ps(s). | Psalm(s) |
| Num. | Numbers | | Prov. | Proverbs |
| Deut. | Deuteronomy | | Eccles. | Ecclesiastes |
| Josh. | Joshua | | Song | Song of Songs |
| Judg. | Judges | | Isa. | Isaiah |
| Ruth | Ruth | | Jer. | Jeremiah |
| 1 Sam. | 1 Samuel | | Lam. | Lamentations |
| 2 Sam. | 2 Samuel | | Ezek. | Ezekiel |
| 1 Kings | 1 Kings | | Dan. | Daniel |
| 2 Kings | 2 Kings | | Hosea | Hosea |
| 1 Chron. | 1 Chronicles | | Joel | Joel |
| 2 Chron. | 2 Chronicles | | Amos | Amos |
| Ezra | Ezra | | Obad. | Obadiah |
| Neh. | Nehemiah | | Jon. | Jonah |

| Mic. | Micah | Hag. | Haggai |
|------|-------|------|--------|
| Nah. | Nahum | Zech. | Zechariah |
| Hab. | Habakkuk | Mal. | Malachi |
| Zeph. | Zephaniah | | |

## New Testament

| Matt. | Matthew | 1 Tim. | 1 Timothy |
|-------|---------|--------|-----------|
| Mark | Mark | 2 Tim. | 2 Timothy |
| Luke | Luke | Titus | Titus |
| John | John | Philem. | Philemon |
| Acts | Acts | Heb. | Hebrews |
| Rom. | Romans | James | James |
| 1 Cor. | 1 Corinthians | 1 Pet. | 1 Peter |
| 2 Cor. | 2 Corinthians | 2 Pet. | 2 Peter |
| Gal. | Galatians | 1 John | 1 John |
| Eph. | Ephesians | 2 John | 2 John |
| Phil. | Philippians | 3 John | 3 John |
| Col. | Colossians | Jude | Jude |
| 1 Thess. | 1 Thessalonians | Rev. | Revelation |
| 2 Thess. | 2 Thessalonians | | |

## Other Jewish and Christian Sources

| 3 Bar. | 3 Baruch (Greek Apocalypse) |
|--------|------------------------------|
| Herm. Mand. | Shepherd of Hermas, Mandate(s) |
| Ign. *Smyrn.* | Ignatius, *To the Smyrnaeans* |
| Let. Aris. | Letter of Aristeas |
| 1 Macc. | 1 Maccabees |
| Sib. Or. | Sibylline Oracles |

# 1

# KOINE GREEK

## Matthew 18:8

### Introduction

It is commonly thought that the most literal translation of the Bible is the best version. In other words, whatever the Greek says should be rendered straightforwardly and without addition or subtraction in the receptor language. But translating the Bible with such a wooden understanding of translation theory is doomed to produce less than ideal results. Because language is complex and ever changing, we must allow for a more nuanced view of how the Bible should be translated. For example, Matthew 18:8 states, "If your hand or your foot causes you to sin, cut it off and throw it away. It is better for you to enter life crippled or lame than with two hands or two feet to be thrown into the eternal fire." The Greek term translated "better" (καλόν) is the positive adjective ordinarily meaning "good." But is Jesus really stating that it is "good" to enter eternal life maimed or lame?

### Overview

In the early part of the twentieth century, it was common for Christians to claim that the Greek of the NT was a special Spirit-inspired Greek and thus different from the typical Greek of the first century.

Then scholars compared NT Greek with the Greek found in various papyri of the time and discovered that the NT used the common (colloquial or popular) Greek of the day.[1] That is, the Greek of the NT is closer to the language of the ordinary person than to that of the educated person who wrote literature for others to read (e.g., Plutarch).[2] And yet the Greek of the NT is still somewhat unique.[3] Its uniqueness is probably due to at least two factors. First, the NT authors were heavily influenced by the Septuagint (i.e., the Greek translation of the OT). This influence is seen not only when the Septuagint is quoted but also in the syntax and sentence structure. Second, the NT authors were influenced by the reality of the gospel, and along with that came the need to express themselves in new ways. Machen explains: "They had come under the influence of new convictions of a transforming kind, and those new convictions had their effect in the sphere of language. Common words had to be given new and loftier meanings."[4]

The Greek language used during the time of the writing of the NT is known as Koine (common) Greek (300 BC–AD 330). Before this era, the Greek language is known as Classical Greek (800–500 BC) and Ionic-Attic Greek (500–300 BC). Many significant changes occurred in the transition from the Classical/Attic Greek to Koine Greek. Here are some of those changes:

- The increased use of prepositions rather than cases alone to communicate the relationship between words (e.g., Eph. 1:5, προορίσας ἡμᾶς <u>εἰς</u> υἱοθεσίαν <u>διὰ</u> Ἰησοῦ Χριστοῦ <u>εἰς</u> αὑτόν, <u>κατὰ</u> τὴν εὐδοκίαν τοῦ θελήματος αὐτοῦ, "He predestined us <u>to</u> adoption as sons <u>through</u> Jesus Christ <u>to</u> Himself, <u>according to</u> the kind intention of His will," NASB), as well as a lack of precision between prepositions (e.g., διά/ἐκ [Rom. 3:30], ἐν/εἰς or περί/ὑπέρ).

1. See esp. Adolf Deissmann, *Light from the Ancient East: The New Testament Illustrated by Recently Discovered Texts of the Graeco-Roman World*, trans. Lionel R. M. Strachan (Peabody, MA: Hendrickson, 1995; German original 1909).
2. J. Gresham Machen states, "Undoubtedly the language of the New Testament is no artificial language of books, and no Jewish-Greek jargon, but the natural, living language of the period." *New Testament Greek for Beginners* (Toronto: Macmillan, 1923), 5.
3. Wallace (28) summarizes, "The *style* is Semitic, the *syntax* is conversational/literary Koine (the descendant of Attic), and the *vocabulary* is vernacular Koine."
4. Machen, *New Testament Greek for Beginners*, 5.

- The decreased use of the optative mood (found only 68 times in the NT). Most occurrences are found in formulaic constructions such as μὴ γένοιτο ("May it never be!" NASB; used 14 times by Paul and once by Luke) and εἴη ("could be"; used 11 times by Luke and once by John).

- The spelling change of certain verbs such as first-aorist endings applied to second-aorist verbs (εἶπαν instead of εἶπον, "they said") and omega-verb endings found on some μι verbs (ἀφίουσιν instead of ἀφιέασιν, "they allow/forgive").

- The increase of shorter, simpler sentences and as well as the increase of coordinated clauses (parataxis).

And the change that we will focus on in this chapter:

- *The increased use of positive and comparative adjective forms used to express a superlative or elative idea.*

## Interpretation

This last change in Koine helps us understand a number of passages, particularly why they often are not translated "literally." In Matthew 18:8, is Jesus really stating that it is "good" (καλόν) for someone to enter eternal life maimed or lame? The answer is obviously no, since it is not necessarily "good" for a person to enter eternal life that way, but it is "better" to enter that way than not at all. Thus, here a positive adjective is used in place of a comparative adjective, a common feature in Koine Greek. This interpretation is confirmed by comparing this passage with a similar saying of Jesus earlier in Matthew's Gospel. In Matthew 5:29–30, συμφέρει (it is profitable, it is better) is used instead of καλόν . . . ἐστίν (it is good).

Another reason we know that the positive adjective can function as a comparative (or superlative) and that a comparative can function as a superlative is that it is fairly common and is sometimes found in contexts where the adjective *must* function in a way that is different from its "normal" meaning. For example, in Matthew 22:38 we read, αὕτη ἐστὶν ἡ μεγάλη καὶ πρώτη ἐντολή (literally, "This is the great and first commandment"). Although there is not consistency among the English Bible versions in translating this verse, it seems best to translate the positive adjective μεγάλη (great) as a superlative adjective (greatest). This interpretation is derived from the fact that it is one commandment among many (as is confirmed by the use of "first" and "second" in the context). So, for example, the NRSV translates the verse as follows: "This is the greatest and first commandment" (see also CSB, NET, NJB, NLT).[5] Another example is found in 1 Corinthians 13:13, where Paul writes, νυνὶ δὲ μένει πίστις, ἐλπίς, ἀγάπη, τὰ τρία ταῦτα· μείζων δὲ τούτων ἡ ἀγάπη, "So now faith, hope, and love abide, these three; but the greatest of these is love." Here Paul uses the comparative adjective μείζων (greater). The problem, however, is that a comparative adjective is normally used where there are only two entities and one is given a greater degree than the other. So, for example, love is considered *greater* than faith. But in 1 Corinthians 13:13 Paul offers three concepts: (1) faith, (2) hope, and (3) love. When more than two concepts are compared, a superlative adjective becomes necessary (at least in English). But because Paul uses a comparative adjective when a superlative is typically used, this clearly demonstrates the use of a comparative for a superlative.

One more item should be mentioned here. It was common for a positive adjective to function as a comparative or superlative and for a comparative adjective to function as a superlative. It was *not* common, however, for a comparative adjective to function as a positive or for a superlative adjective to function as a comparative or positive. The diagram illustrates that an adjective could perform the function of the adjective degree above it, but not (usually) below it.

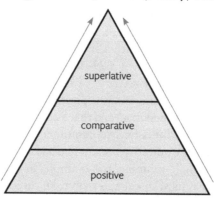

5. So also Charles L. Quarles, *Matthew*, EGGNT (Nashville: B&H, 2017), 265.

# 2

# TEXTUAL CRITICISM

## Romans 5:1

### Introduction

Paul's letter to the Christians at Rome is arguably the greatest letter ever written.[1] As John Stott declares, "It is the fullest, plainest and grandest statement of the gospel in the New Testament."[2] And while there is no doubt that the apostle Paul is the author of the epistle, there are a few places where there is some debate as to precisely what Paul wrote. For example, in Romans 5:1 we read, "Therefore, since we have been justified by faith, we have [ἔχομεν] peace with God through our Lord Jesus Christ." But some scholars, such as Stanley Porter, have argued that this verse should be rendered, "Therefore, since we have been justified by faith, let us have [ἔχωμεν] peace with God through our Lord Jesus Christ." On what basis does Porter make this claim?[3]

1. See Benjamin L. Merkle, "Is Romans Really the Greatest Letter Ever Written?," *SBJT* 11, no. 3 (2007): 18–32.
2. John R. W. Stott, *The Message of Romans*, Bible Speaks Today (Leicester, UK: Inter-Varsity, 1994), 19.
3. Stanley E. Porter, "Not Only That (οὐ μόνον), but It Has Been Said Before: A Response to Verlyn Verbrugge, or Why Reading Previous Scholarship Can Avoid Scholarly Misunderstandings," *JETS* 56, no. 3 (2013): 577–83.

## Overview

The answer to Porter's claim has to do with textual criticism. Textual criticism is the study of determining which textual variant is most likely the original reading. Because the original manuscripts (autographs) have not survived, we are dependent on copies of the originals. The problem arises when the copies have slight differences (i.e., variants). Today we have access to nearly 6,000 NT Greek manuscripts that date from AD 125 to the sixteenth century. In seeking to determine the most likely reading, it is important to consider both external and internal evidence.

*External evidence* relates to the age, location, and quantity of the manuscripts that support a particular variant. Below are a few general principles for judging the external evidence:

- *Prefer the older manuscripts.* It is assumed that the older a manuscript is, the less time it had for errors to creep in. Conversely, the younger a manuscript is, the further separated in time it is from the original and thus the more chance it had for errors to be introduced into the manuscript. Thus manuscripts often favored include ℵ (Sinaiticus, 4th cent.), A (Alexandrinus, 5th cent.), B (Vaticanus, 4th cent.), C (Ephraemi Rescriptus, 5th cent.), and the portion of D containing the Pauline Epistles (Claromontanus, 6th cent.).
- *Prefer the reading that is supported by the majority of (significant) manuscripts.* Because the majority of manuscripts come from the Byzantine tradition, this criterion must be qualified by the term "significant." Most of the manuscripts we possess today are labeled "Byzantine" since Greek continued to be used in the East while Latin remained dominant in the West. Hence the great majority of these manuscripts follow the Byzantine reading, but they are often relatively young manuscripts (8th–15th cent.). These later manuscripts are often not considered significant since they come from an earlier exemplar.[4] Thus manuscripts must be weighed and not merely counted.

4. An exemplar is a text used to produce another text.

- *Prefer the reading that is best attested across various families of manuscripts.* There are three main families of manuscripts based on geographic provenance: (1) Byzantine, (2) Alexandrian, and (3) Western. The manuscripts in these families often display a family resemblance, which indicates a common source. The Alexandrian family (which includes ℵ, A, B, C)[5] is often considered the most reliable. A disputed reading that includes manuscripts from several families is considered significant.

*Internal evidence* relates to the context of where the disputed variants are found. That is, how do the variants relate to the author's style, theology, and argumentation in the larger context? Below are a few general principles of how to judge the internal evidence:

- *Prefer the reading that best corresponds with the style and theology of the author.* Because various authors tend to use somewhat predictable stylistic patterns and embrace certain theological motifs, it is important to take those characteristics into account. We must remember, however, that these features can change due to differences in (1) an amanuensis (ancient secretary), (2) purpose, or (3) recipient.
- *Prefer the reading that best explains the origin of the other variants.* This is perhaps the most important internal criterion since it leads us to examine what might have caused the variant in the first place. Thus it is helpful to ask, "Which reading might have caused the variant reading?" Knowing scribal tendencies helps answer this question.
- *Prefer the more difficult reading.* Because scribes tended to "fix" or "improve" texts, it is best to choose the harder reading. In other words, it is more likely that a scribe sought to clarify a text rather than introduce confusion and difficulty into a text.
- *Prefer the shorter reading.* Because scribes tended to clarify or explain a text, it is best to choose the more abbreviated

5. The Gospels in Codices A and B are considered part of the Byzantine textual tradition.

reading. This is especially true when investigating parallel passages in the Synoptic Gospels.[6]

## Interpretation

Based on the above information, which reading is to be preferred in Romans 5:1? Let's review the text: δικαιωθέντες οὖν ἐκ πίστεως εἰρήνην ἔχομεν [ἔχωμεν] πρὸς τὸν θεὸν διὰ τοῦ κυρίου ἡμῶν Ἰησοῦ Χριστοῦ, "Therefore, since we have been justified by faith, we have [let us have] peace with God through our Lord Jesus Christ." The difference between the two variants is that some manuscripts have an indicative form (ἔχομεν), whereas others have a (hortatory) subjunctive form (ἔχωμεν).

Based on the external evidence, the subjunctive form should be preferred. It is found in the majority of the earliest manuscripts (אּ*, A, B*, C, and D)[7] and is represented by various families (Byzantine: K, L; Alexandrian: אּ*, A, B*, C, 33, and 81; and Western: D). In contrast, the indicative reading is supported by אּ¹, B², F, G, P, and Ψ.[8] With external evidence this strong, why is it that virtually no English version opts for the subjunctive reading? The answer is that the internal evidence in this case is seen to outweigh the external evidence.[9]

---

6. For a standard work on textual criticism, see Bruce M. Metzger and Bart D. Ehrman, *The Text of the New Testament: Its Transmission, Corruption, and Restoration*, 4th ed. (New York: Oxford University Press, 2005). See also David Alan Black, *New Testament Textual Criticism: A Concise Guide* (Grand Rapids: Baker, 1994); Black, ed., *Rethinking New Testament Textual Criticism* (Grand Rapids: Baker Academic, 2002); Michael Holmes, "Textual Criticism," in *New Testament Criticism and Interpretation*, ed. David Alan Black and David S. Dockery (Grand Rapids: Zondervan, 1991), 100–134; KMP 24–35; Arthur G. Patzia, *The Making of the New Testament: Origin, Collection, and Canon*, 2nd ed. (Downers Grove, IL: IVP Academic, 2011), 229–47; Daniel B. Wallace, ed., *Revisiting the Corruption of the New Testament: Manuscript, Patristic, and Apocryphal Evidence* (Grand Rapids: Kregel, 2011).

7. An asterisk (*) next to the letter of the manuscript indicates the original reading (since the manuscript was later "corrected").

8. The superscripted ¹ and ² indicate successive correctors of a manuscript.

9. Bruce M. Metzger notes that although the subjunctive form has better external evidence, "a majority of the Committee judge that internal evidence must here take precedence." *A Textual Commentary on the Greek New Testament*, 2nd ed. (Stuttgart: United Bible Societies, 1994), 452.

Based on the internal evidence, the indicative form is preferred.[10] Although the subjunctive is considered the more difficult reading, for many it is viewed as too difficult. In addition, the indicative best corresponds with the context and with Paul's theology. Metzger (*Textual Commentary*, 452) explains: "Since in this passage it appears that Paul is not exhorting but stating facts ('peace' is the possession of those who have been justified), only the indicative is consonant with the apostle's argument." In this case, the internal evidence is given priority because the difference between the two readings is probably due to the similar pronunciation between the omicron and the omega in the Hellenistic age. Additionally, Metzger and Ehrman assert that the more difficult reading should be viewed as "relative, and a point is sometimes reached when a reading must be judged to be so difficult that it can have arisen only by accident in transcription."[11]

In the end, the difference between the indicative and the subjunctive is small in light of the entire epistle. As Verbrugge summarizes, "Regardless of whether Paul makes a statement ('we have peace with God'), or . . . an outright exhortation ('let us enjoy the peace we have with God'), the truth remains that through the saving work of Christ, who is our peace (Eph. 2:14), we do have peace with God."[12]

10. For a defense of this position, see Verlyn D. Verbrugge, "The Grammatical Internal Evidence for ἔχωμεν in Romans 5:1," *JETS* 54, no. 3 (2011): 559–72.
11. Metzger and Ehrman, *Text of the New Testament*, 303.
12. Verbrugge, "Grammatical Internal Evidence," 572.

# 3

# NOMINATIVE CASE

## John 1:1

### Introduction

Recently, a student came to my office to discuss the Greek course he was taking with me that semester. During our conversation, he asked me about John 1:1 since his mother-in-law is a Jehovah's Witness. The *New World Translation*, the official Bible translation of Jehovah's Witnesses, states, "In the beginning was the Word, and the Word was with God, and the Word was a god." In Greek, the last phrase reads καὶ θεὸς ἦν ὁ λόγος. It is well known that the nominative noun θεός lacks the definite article. So, does this mean that the Jehovah's Witness interpretation of this passage is valid, or is such an interpretation the result of defective theology and/or a misuse of grammar?

### Overview

The nominative case is used most frequently to designate the subject of the verb. There are, however, several other functions of the nominative case. Here are some of the key uses:

- *Subject* (the subject of the finite verb): "The Father [ὁ πατήρ] loves the Son" (John 3:35).

- *Predicate nominative* (expresses a characteristic or state of the subject with a copulative verb): "The life was the light [τὸ φῶς] of men" (John 1:4).
- *Apposition* (provides additional information about a subject): "Paul, an apostle [ἀπόστολος] of Christ Jesus" (Col. 1:1).
- *Absolute* (grammatically independent and often used in greetings): "The grace [ἡ χάρις] of our Lord Jesus Christ be with you all" (2 Thess. 3:18).
- *Address* (used instead of a vocative): "Husbands [οἱ ἄνδρες], love your wives" (Col. 3:19).

Most verbs take a direct object in the accusative case. With a predicate nominative, however, both the subject *and* the predicate nominative are in the nominative case. Such constructions contain a stated or implied usage of an equative verb (such as εἰμί, γίνομαι, or ὑπάρχω). A predicate nominative provides further information about the subject and may be virtually equivalent to the subject. But if both the subject and the predicate nominative are in the nominative case, how do we determine which is the subject? Wallace (42–46) offers the following guidelines:

1. If there is a pronoun (whether stated or embedded in the verb), it is the subject.
2. If one of the nominatives is articular, it is the subject.
3. If one of the nominatives is a proper name, it is the subject.

Furthermore, Wallace lists a "pecking" order for when both nouns have one of these qualities: the pronoun has the highest priority; articular nouns and proper names have an equal authority.

### Interpretation

In the example of John 1:1, because "the word" (ὁ λόγος) has the article and "God" (θεός) lacks the article, "the word" is clearly the subject. But the question remains as to why θεός lacks the article (i.e., is anarthrous). There are several reasons why θεός should not be translated as "a god" but instead refers to the full deity of Jesus as God, the Second Person of the Trinity:

1. John has already stated, "in the beginning was the Word" (John 1:1) and will go on to claim that "all things were made through him" (John 1:3). Genesis 1:1 states, "In the beginning, God created the heavens and the earth." This parallel implies that Jesus is indeed the Creator.

2. As a Jew, John was firmly committed to monotheism. Consequently, it is highly unlikely that he would have referred to another person as "a god."

3. The inclusion of the article would have stated something different than John intended. Carson explains: "In fact, if John had included the article, he would have been saying something quite untrue. He would have been so identifying the Word with God that no divine being could exist apart from the Word."[1] In essence, if John had written καὶ ὁ λόγος ἦν ὁ θεός, he would have been affirming what was later named Sabellianism—the heresy that equated Christ with God so that there is no distinction of person. Such an understanding also contradicts John's earlier statement where he proclaims that "the Word was *with* (πρός) God." The preposition πρός in this context indicates personal relationship.[2] Indeed, if Christ and God the Father are equated, the phrase becomes meaningless since one person cannot be "with" himself.

4. In NT Greek syntax, when the predicate nominative *precedes* the verb, it typically lacks the article whether it was considered indefinite or not (i.e., Colwell's Canon). In other words, the grammatical construction determines that the article is lacking, but only the *context* determines whether the noun should be considered indefinite. Furthermore, in this type of construction the predicate nominative "is normally qualitative, sometimes definite, and only rarely indefinite" (Wallace 262).

1. D. A. Carson, *The Gospel according to John*, PNTC (Grand Rapids: Eerdmans, 1991), 117.
2. See BDF §239.1, p. 125; Edward W. Klink III, *John*, ZECNT (Grand Rapids: Zondervan, 2016), 91.

5. The anarthrous use of θεός is found in the immediate context and is still considered definite. Interestingly, even the *New World Translation* renders these occurrences as definite, demonstrating its inconsistency:[3]

- "There came a man who was sent as a representative of God [θεοῦ]; his name was John" (John 1:6).
- "However, to all who did receive him, he gave authority to become God's [θεοῦ] children" (John 1:12).
- "And they were born, not from blood or from a fleshly will or from man's will, but from God [θεοῦ]" (John 1:13).
- "No man has seen God [θεόν] at any time" (John 1:18).

Each of these four examples occurs in the immediate context of John 1:1, and yet the anarthrous use of θεός is never translated as "a god." Additionally, the same argument could be made regarding the translation of other terms in the context that are anarthrous yet still translated as definite: ἐν ἀρχῇ, "in *the* beginning" (John 1:1, 2); ζωή, "life" (John 1:4).

6. If John wanted to communicate that Jesus was merely "a god" or "divine," he could have stated that Jesus was θεῖος ("divine"; cf. Acts 17:29; 2 Pet. 1:3, 4).

7. The notion that Jesus is indeed God is consistent with John's descriptions of Jesus elsewhere in his Gospel. That is, the titles, works, and attributes found in the Gospel of John affirm Jesus's deity (see, e.g., John 5:23; 8:58; 10:30). Indeed, the articular use of θεός with reference to Jesus is found in John 20:28, where Thomas confesses, "My Lord and my God!" (ὁ κύριός μου καὶ ὁ θεός μου).

Thus John 1:1 "is very carefully constructed to refer to the personal distinctness yet the essential oneness of the Word with God."[4] The Word (Jesus) shares all the attributes of God (the Father) but is

---

3. In fact, R. H. Countess has demonstrated that of the 282 anarthrous uses of θεός, the *New World Translation* renders the term indefinite only 16 times, or only 6 percent of the time. *The Jehovah's Witnesses' New Testament: A Critical Analysis of the "New World Translation of the Christian Greek Scriptures"* (Philipsburg, NJ: Presbyterian and Reformed, 1982), 54–55.

4. Rodney A. Whitacre, *John*, IVPNTCS (Downers Grove, IL: InterVarsity, 1999), 50.

a distinct person. Thus the Greek use of the predicate nominative is qualitative: Jesus possesses the essence of the Father but is not identified as the Father. Wallace (269) summarizes: "The construction the evangelist chose to express this idea was the most *concise* way he could have stated that the Word was God and yet was distinct from the Father." The Nicene Creed helpfully clarifies and affirms the nature of Jesus's humanity and his deity:

> We believe in . . . one Lord Jesus Christ, the Son of God, the begotten of God the Father, the Only-begotten, that is of the essence of the Father. God of God, Light of Light, true God of true God, begotten and not made; of the very same nature [*homoousion*] of the Father, by Whom all things came into being, in heaven and on earth, visible and invisible. Who for us humanity and for our salvation came down from heaven, was incarnate, was made human, was born perfectly of the holy virgin Mary by the Holy Spirit. By whom He took body, soul, and mind, and everything that is in man, truly and not in semblance. He suffered, was crucified, was buried, rose again on the third day, ascended into heaven with the same body, [and] sat at the right hand of the Father. He is to come with the same body and with the glory of the Father, to judge the living and the dead; of His kingdom there is no end.[5]

5. http://www.armenianchurchlibrary.com/files/creed.pdf.

# 4

# VOCATIVE CASE

## Ephesians 5:21–22

### Introduction

In Ephesians 5:21 Paul exhorts his readers, "Submit to one another out of reverence for Christ" (NIV). It is well known, however, that the Greek word translated "submit" is actually a dependent adverbial participle (ὑποτασσόμενοι) that is better translated "submitting." Consequently, verse 21 is closely associated with the preceding context. For example, Roberts comments that although many English versions begin a new sentence in verse 21, "in the Greek text, [ὑποτασσόμενοι] is a participle, ('submitting') that depends grammatically on the imperative ('be filled'). Thus, verse 21 completes the exhortation that began in verse 18."[1]

---

This chapter is a summary of my earlier work, "The Start of Instruction to Wives and Husbands—Ephesians 5:21 or 5:22?," *BSac* 174, no. 694 (April–June 2017): 179–92.

1. Mark D. Roberts, *Ephesians*, Story of God Bible Commentary (Grand Rapids: Zondervan, 2016), 193–94. See also Markus Barth, *Ephesians 4–6*, AB 34A (Garden City, NY: Doubleday, 1974), 608.

Ephesians 5:18–22

| NA²⁸ | UBS⁵ | SBLGNT |
|---|---|---|
| ¹⁸... **πληροῦσθε** ἐν πνεύματι, ¹⁹<u>λαλοῦντες</u>... ᾄδοντες καὶ ψάλλοντες, ...²⁰<u>εὐχαριστοῦντες</u> πάντοτε ὑπὲρ πάντων ἐν ὀνόματι τοῦ κυρίου ἡμῶν Ἰησοῦ Χριστοῦ τῷ θεῷ καὶ πατρί. ²¹<u>Ὑποτασσόμενοι</u> ἀλλήλοις ἐν φόβῳ Χριστοῦ, ²²αἱ γυναῖκες τοῖς ἰδίοις ἀνδράσιν ὡς τῷ κυρίῳ. | ¹⁸... **πληροῦσθε** ἐν πνεύματι, ¹⁹<u>λαλοῦντες</u>... ᾄδοντες καὶ ψάλλοντες, ...²⁰<u>εὐχαριστοῦντες</u> πάντοτε ὑπὲρ πάντων ἐν ὀνόματι τοῦ κυρίου ἡμῶν Ἰησοῦ Χριστοῦ τῷ θεῷ καὶ πατρί. **Wives and Husbands** ²¹<u>Ὑποτασσόμενοι</u> ἀλλήλοις ἐν φόβῳ Χριστοῦ, ²²αἱ γυναῖκες τοῖς ἰδίοις ἀνδράσιν ὡς τῷ κυρίῳ. | ¹⁸... **πληροῦσθε** ἐν πνεύματι, ¹⁹<u>λαλοῦντες</u>... ᾄδοντες καὶ ψάλλοντες, ...²⁰<u>εὐχαριστοῦντες</u> πάντοτε ὑπὲρ πάντων ἐν ὀνόματι τοῦ κυρίου ἡμῶν Ἰησοῦ Χριστοῦ τῷ θεῷ καὶ πατρί, ²¹<u>ὑποτασσόμενοι</u> ἀλλήλοις ἐν φόβῳ Χριστοῦ. ²²Αἱ γυναῖκες τοῖς ἰδίοις ἀνδράσιν ὡς τῷ κυρίῳ. |

If that is the case, why do the NA²⁸, UBS⁵, and many major English versions add a sentence and even a paragraph break before verse 21 (see table), especially in light of the best grammatical and syntactical evidence? More to the point, what evidence is there that verse 21 concludes the previous section more than introducing the next section? One key answer to this question involves the vocative case.

## Overview

The vocative case often occurs at the beginning of a sentence or clause and indicates the person (or group) that is being addressed. Although there is some question as to whether the vocative qualifies as a distinct case (especially since it often overlaps with the nominative case in the plural forms), it seems best to treat it as such. The vocative conveys direct address, with or without the article and sometimes with the inflectional particle ὦ, which may indicate additional emphasis or deep emotion.² The most common distinct ending in the vocative case is -ε (e.g., κύριε).

2. The inflectional particle ὦ is used in conjunction with the vocative seventeen times in the NT. Regarding the function of ὦ, Zerwick (*Bib. Gk.*, §35, p. 12) notes, "This is but a little particle, but it casts such a light on the state of mind of our Lord

## Interpretation

Many Bible versions and commentators divide the text between Ephesians 5:20 and 5:21, with verse 21 beginning a new sentence (or paragraph) related to wives and husbands. If a new paragraph begins at verse 21, then this verse can be viewed as the heading for verses 22–33 and therefore is sometimes viewed as the interpretive grid through which the rest of the text is to be understood. In other words, verse 21—which calls for mutual submission, "Submit to one another"—is often seen as the governing verse of the entire passage. The main reasons for this position include (1) the independent (imperatival) function of the participle (ὑποτασσόμενοι) in verse 21, (2) the common themes of submission and fear in verses 21–33, and (3) the lack of a verb in verse 22 ("submitting" is inferred from verse 21).

Others prefer to break the text after verse 21. This is the view of Hoehner, who states, "This verse is not the beginning of a new section but a fitting conclusion . . . to the section which deals with the filling by the Spirit beginning with 5:18."[3] There are several reasons as to why this interpretation is to be preferred, including (1) the dependent (adverbial) use of the participle; (2) the textual variants in verse 22; and, most important for this chapter, (3) the use of a vocative to introduce a new section.

The first reason to make the break after verse 21 is that it is almost certain that the participle "submitting" (ὑποτασσόμενοι) is dependent on the imperative "be filled" (πληροῦσθε) in verse 18 and, as such, is not an independent verb. If the break is made before verse 21, then the participle functions imperatively, which is a very rare usage.[4] As a general rule, when there is doubt, it is better to view a participle as dependent on the main verb (adverbial) as opposed to an independent imperatival participle.[5] It is best, therefore, to interpret

---

and of His apostles, that no one, surely, in reading the Scriptures, would wish to neglect its indications."

3. Harold W. Hoehner, *Ephesians: An Exegetical Commentary* (Grand Rapids: Baker Academic, 2002), 716; see also Ernest Best, *Ephesians*, ICC (London: T&T Clark, 1998), 517.

4. Wallace 639, 659n6; G. B. Winer, *A Grammar of the Idiom of the New Testament*, trans. and rev. W. F. Moulton, 7th ed. (Andover, MA: Draper, 1892), 351.

5. Robertson 1133–34; B&W 138; Steven E. Runge, *Discourse Grammar of the Greek New Testament* (Peabody, MA: Hendrickson, 2010), 266–67; Wallace 651.

the participle as adverbial, modifying πληροῦσθε (v. 18), communicating result (Wallace 639; Young 157). Indeed, ὑποτασσόμενοι is the last of the string of five anarthrous (present tense-form) participles that all describe what it looks like when someone is filled by the Spirit. To break the text before the last participle seems somewhat arbitrary. As such, this participle should not be construed as imperatival and certainly not as beginning a new sentence.

A second reason to break the text after verse 21 relates to the textual variants found in verse 22. The NA and UBS texts omit the imperatival form of ὑποτάσσω from verse 22 since it is not found in some early manuscripts. The verb ὑποτάσσεσθε (imperative, "[you all] submit") is lacking in 𝔓⁴⁶ (ca. AD 200), B (Vaticanus), and a few early fathers but is included after γυναῖκες in D, F, and G and after ἀνδράσιν in most Byzantine text-types.⁶ The alternate form ὑποτασσέσθωσαν (imperative, "Let them submit") is found after γυναῖκες in Ψ and after ἀνδράσιν in ℵ (Sinaiticus), A (Alexandrinus), and other significant manuscripts. The UBS committee preferred the shorter reading because it "accords with the succinct style of the author's admonitions, and explained the other readings as expansions introduced for the sake of clarity, the main verb being required especially when the words Αἱ γυναῖκες stood at the beginning of a scripture lesson."⁷

My point here is not to argue for or against the verb's inclusion (though I think the original probably lacked the verb).⁸ Rather, these variants demonstrate that earlier Christians often favored breaking the text after verse 21. The verb was probably added because the new section was thought to begin at verse 22, and so a verb was supplied. The additional verb would have been especially helpful for lectionary readings.⁹ Not surprisingly, most manuscripts include an imperative to solve this apparent difficulty since there are imperatives in

6. The form ὑποτάσσεσθε is also found in Col. 3:18, which makes it a bit suspicious here because it suggests that a scribe may have unwittingly harmonized the wording of the two passages.
7. Bruce M. Metzger, *A Textual Commentary on the Greek New Testament*, 2nd ed. (Stuttgart: United Bible Societies, 1994), 541.
8. Most commentators favor its omission. For an exception, see Hoehner, *Ephesians*, 730–31.
9. Best, *Ephesians*, 531; J. Armitage Robinson, *St Paul's Epistle to the Ephesians*, 2nd ed. (London: Macmillan, 1914), 204.

5:25 (ἀγαπᾶτε), 6:1 (ὑπακούετε), and 6:5 (ὑπακούετε), as well as an imperative in the parallel passage in Colossians 3:18 (ὑποτάσσεσθε; cf. 1 Pet. 3:1). Thus the addition of a verb in verse 22 in most manuscripts suggests that the text was often read independently of its preceding context.

A final reason to view the break after verse 21 is that verse 22 begins with the vocative (αἱ γυναῖκες, technically a nominative used as a vocative or a nominative of address).[10] As is often the case, the vocative signals the start of a new section (Young 253). This usage is confirmed by the use of the vocative in the following paragraphs, which begin the new sections with the vocatives "children" (τὰ τέκνα, 6:1) and "slaves" (οἱ δοῦλοι, 6:5).[11]

In addition, the lack of a conjunction (asyndeton) may also signify a break in the text.[12] Levinsohn writes that asyndeton "is commonly found at the beginning of a new paragraph or section if that unit has its own nucleus," adding that "the absence of a conjunction is significant only in connection with other potential boundary features such as *vocatives*."[13] Thus the combination of asyndeton with the vocative adds a further indication that there is a break in the text.

Thus, although the NA[28], UBS[5], and many English versions insert a sentence (or even paragraph) break before verse 21, the grammar and syntax make it evident that verse 21 is more closely linked with the preceding context.

Our understanding of the structure of this passage can influence our interpretation of it (especially the meaning and nature of

10. BDF §147.3, pp. 81–82; Wallace 58.
11. See Runge, *Discourse Grammar*, 117–18.
12. Runge, *Discourse Grammar*, 20–23. See also Winer, *Grammar*, 537; Robertson 428, 440; Herbert Weir Smyth and Gordon M. Messing, *Greek Grammar*, rev. ed. (Cambridge, MA: Harvard University Press, 1966), 484–85; BDF §458, pp. 239–40; Wallace 658; Stephen H. Levinsohn, "Some Constraints on Discourse Development in the Pastoral Epistles," in *Discourse Analysis and the New Testament: Approaches and Results*, ed. Stanley E. Porter and Jeffrey T. Reed, JSNTSup 170 (Sheffield: Sheffield Academic, 1999), 318, 330; Stephanie L. Black, *Sentence Conjunctions in the Gospel of Matthew: καί, δέ, τότε, γάρ, οὖν and Asyndeton in Narrative Discourse*, JSNTSup 216 (Sheffield: Sheffield Academic, 2002), 182.
13. Stephen H. Levinsohn, *Discourse Features of New Testament Greek: A Coursebook on the Information Structure of New Testament Greek*, 2nd ed. (Dallas: SIL International, 2000), 276; see also 118, 278.

submission in vv. 22–33), and vice versa, our interpretation of the passage can influence how we view its structure. As Klyne Snodgrass remarks, "Failure to understand the structure [of this passage] has made this section one of the most misappropriated texts in the Bible."[14]

---

14. Klyne Snodgrass, *Ephesians*, NIVAC (Grand Rapids: Zondervan, 1996), 286.

# 5

# GENITIVE CASE

## 1 Timothy 3:6

## Introduction

The genitive case is the most flexible of the Greek cases in that it has a broader range of functions than the other cases. In a given context such syntactical possibilities decrease greatly since it is the context that determines the particular function of a case. In most instances, identifying the particular use of a genitive is easy enough and is not a matter of debate. There are, however, some verses that remain open to interpretation. For example, in 1 Timothy 3:6 Paul insists that new overseers of the church should not be recent converts; otherwise such candidates might become puffed up with pride and fall into "the condemnation of the devil" (κρίμα τοῦ διαβόλου). But does this genitive construction mean "the condemnation that the devil gives" or "the condemnation that the devil receives"? Both are grammatical and syntactical possibilities arising from the use of the genitive case.

## Overview

The genitive is often designated as the case of restriction, description, or separation. While the accusative case restricts verbs, the genitive case restricts or limits nouns, often denoting a quality of a person or thing (thus similar to an adjective). For example, "the birth of Jesus Christ" (τοῦ Ἰησοῦ Χριστοῦ ἡ γένεσις, Matt. 1:18) specifies whose birth is referred to, and "the Father of glory" (ὁ πατὴρ τῆς δόξης, Eph. 1:17) is best understood as an attributive (adjectival) genitive meaning "glorious father." In most cases the word "of" is used in English translation, though it is far too simplistic always to use this term to express the relationship between the head noun and the genitive term. As seen in the examples below, "from," "in," "by," and "than" (among others) can also be used. Typically the genitive noun follows the noun that it qualifies, though this order is sometimes reversed for emphasis or contrast.

- *Possession* (identifies ownership of the head noun): "he entered the house of God [τοῦ θεοῦ]" = "God's house" (Matt. 12:4).
- *Relationship* (signifies a family relationship, e.g., a parent, spouse, or sibling): "John the brother of James [τοῦ Ἰακώβου]" (Mark 3:17).
- *Attributive* (conveys an attribute or quality of the head noun): "king of righteousness [δικαιοσύνης]" = "righteous king" (Heb. 7:2).
- *Source* (designates the origin of the head noun): "it is a gift from God [θεοῦ]" (Eph. 2:8 NLT).
- *Content or material* (indicates the content of an object or the material of which an object is made): *Content*—"the net full of fish [τῶν ἰχθύων]" (John 21:8); *Material*—"cargo of gold [χρυσοῦ]" (Rev. 18:12).
- *Partitive* (denotes the whole of which the head noun is a part): "one of the prophets [τῶν προφητῶν]" (Matt. 16:14).
- *Subjective* (functions as the subject of the verbal idea implied in the head noun): "In this the love of God [τοῦ θεοῦ] was made manifest among us" (1 John 4:9).
- *Objective* (functions as the direct object of the verbal idea implied in the head noun): "Have faith in God [θεοῦ]" (Mark 11:22).

- *Time* (specifies the kind of time within which an action occurs): "[He] took the child and his mother <u>by night</u> [νυκτός]" (Matt. 2:14).

- *Separation* (indicates movement away from, whether literally or figuratively): "alienated <u>from the commonwealth</u> [τῆς πολιτείας] of Israel" (Eph. 2:12).

- *Comparison* (denotes comparison with a comparative adjective): "For the foolishness of God is wiser <u>than men</u> [τῶν ἀνθρώπων]" (1 Cor. 1:25).

- *Apposition* (provides an alternate designation or explanatory restatement of the head noun): "the gift <u>of the Holy Spirit</u> [τοῦ ἁγίου πνεύματος]" (Acts 2:38).

- *Direct object* (verbs of sensation, emotion or volition, sharing, ruling, or separation can take their direct object in the genitive case): "he desires <u>a noble task</u> [καλοῦ ἔργου]" (1 Tim. 3:1).

Subjective and objective genitives are similar in that they both are typically possible options when the head noun conveys a verbal idea. With the subjective genitive, the head noun functions as the subject of the verbal idea: "love of God" = "God loves someone." With the objective genitive, the head noun functions as the object of the verbal idea: "love of God" = "someone loves God."

### Interpretation

So, in our example mentioned above (1 Tim. 3:6), does "the condemnation of the devil" (κρίμα τοῦ διαβόλου) mean "the condemnation that the devil gives" (subjective genitive)[1] or "the condemnation that the devil receives" (objective genitive)?[2] The first option, the subjective genitive, is certainly possible and is held by some commentators. The

---

1. The subjective genitive is followed by the NET ("the punishment that the devil will exact") and the NLT ("the devil would cause him to fall").
2. The objective genitive is followed by the NIV ("the same judgment as the devil"), NASB ("the condemnation incurred by the devil"), and NKJV/NJB ("the same condemnation as the devil").

arguments in favor of this position are as follows: (1) The parallel genitive construction in the following verse is clearly a subjective genitive.³ Paul mentions that a candidate must have a good testimony with outsiders so that he does not fall into disgrace and "a snare of the devil" (παγίδα τοῦ διαβόλου, 1 Tim. 3:7; cf. 2 Tim. 2:26). Nearly all commentators affirm that this genitive is subjective and refers to the snare set by the devil and not a snare into which the devil fell (i.e., pride). (2) This parallel construction is strengthened by the fact that both verses (1 Tim. 3:6 and 7) refer to the new candidate *falling* (ἐμπέσῃ) into something connected to the devil.

The second option, the objective genitive, is to be preferred for the following reasons: (1) It makes the most sense of the context. Paul warns that an overseer should not be a recent convert since such a person is susceptible to pride, which leads to condemnation, the same condemnation experienced by the devil for his pride. (2) If the genitive in verse 6 is subjective ("the devil condemns"), it would be redundant with verse 7 ("the devil snares"). (3) References to the devil judging or condemning are not common in the NT. In contrast, there are many texts that mention the devil being judged.⁴ Thus it is best to understand 1 Timothy 3:6 as a reference to the condemnation that the devil received. Neophytes should not be considered for leadership in the church since with such authority they can become proud and fall into the same condemnation that the devil received.

---

3. Philip H. Towner notes that "the active role of the devil in 3:7 favors putting him into an active role in this statement." *Letters to Timothy and Titus*, NICNT (Grand Rapids: Eerdmans, 2006), 258.
4. E.g., Matt. 25:41; Luke 10:18; John 16:11; Heb. 2:14; 1 John 3:8; Jude 9; Rev. 12:7–17; 20:7–10; see also Gen. 3:14–15. Luke Timothy Johnson writes, "This interpretation also fits the tradition of the devil as one who is punished because of the arrogance he showed toward God." *The First and Second Letters to Timothy: A New Translation with Introduction and Commentary*, AB 35A (New Haven: Yale University Press, 2001), 217.

# 6

## DATIVE CASE

### Ephesians 5:18

**Introduction**

In Ephesians 5:18 Paul writes: "And do not get drunk with wine, for that is debauchery, but be filled with the Spirit." The first part of the verse is somewhat straightforward: Paul forbids the Ephesian Christians (and by implication us as well) from consuming wine (an alcoholic beverage consisting of one part wine to usually three parts water) so that one becomes intoxicated, thus under its control. But what is meant by the second part of the verse? "Be filled with the Spirit," πληροῦσθε ἐν πνεύματι. Is the Spirit the *content* of what Christians should be filled with, or is the Spirit the *means* by which Christians are filled?

**Overview**

Generally speaking, the dative case limits the action of the verb (1) by specifying the *person* involved (to/for whom?), (2) by designating the *location* of the action (where?), or (3) by indicating the *means* by which an action is accomplished (how?). Overall, the dative case is less ambiguous than the genitive case and is usually easier to classify.

Part of the reason for this distinction is that dative nouns are typically related to verbs, whereas genitive nouns are typically related to other nouns.

- *Indirect object* (indicates the one to or for whom an act is performed): "I give eternal life to them [αὐτοῖς]" (John 10:28 NASB).

- *Advantage or disadvantage* (denotes the person to whose benefit [or detriment] a verbal action occurs): "Do not lay up for yourselves [ὑμῖν] treasures on earth" (Matt. 6:19).

- *Reference/respect* (limits or qualifies the extent of the verbal action): "sound in faith [τῇ πίστει]" (Titus 2:2).

- *Possession* (the dative possesses the subject of an equative verb: εἰμί or γίνομαι): "If a [certain] man [τινι ἀνθρώπῳ] has a hundred sheep . . ." (Matt. 18:12).

- *Sphere/place* (identifies the literal or figurative location): "but made alive in the spirit [πνεύματι]" (1 Pet. 3:18).

- *Time* (indicates the time when the action of a verb is accomplished): "and on the third day [τῇ τρίτῃ ἡμέρᾳ] be raised" (Matt. 16:21).

- *Means* (denotes the impersonal means by which the action of a given verb is accomplished): "He cried out with a loud voice [φωνῇ μεγάλῃ]" (John 11:43).

- *Manner* (signifies the manner in which the action of a given verb is accomplished): "Yet no one was speaking openly [παρρησίᾳ] of Him" (John 7:13 NASB).

- *Agency* (indicates the personal agency by which the action of a given verb is accomplished): "He was . . . seen by angels [ἀγγέλοις]" (1 Tim. 3:16).

- *Association* (denotes the person [or thing] with whom [or which] someone is associated): "[He] made us alive together with Christ [τῷ Χριστῷ]" (Eph. 2:5).

- *Apposition* (provides additional information about a substantive in the dative case): "We always thank God, the Father [πατρί]" (Col. 1:3).

- *Direct object* (verbs of trusting, obeying, serving, worshiping, thanksgiving, or following can take their direct object in the dative case): "They . . . followed him [αὐτῷ]" (Matt. 4:20).

## Interpretation

Most English Bible versions interpret the dative construction in the command to be filled ἐν πνεύματι (Eph. 5:18) as a dative of content (filled *with* the Spirit). Others argue that the text is best understood as a dative of means (filled *by* the Spirit). In other words, is the Spirit that which fills Christians, or is the Spirit the instrument by which Christians are filled?[1] The arguments for interpreting ἐν πνεύματι as a dative of content include the following:[2] (1) The verb πληρόω (or πίμπλημι) can be linked with the dative case to express content.[3] (2) If it is understood as a dative of means, then the content of the filling is left unmentioned. (3) There is a close parallel between the OT concept of the temple being filled with God's presence and the NT concept of believers being filled with God's Spirit (cf. Eph. 2:22).

It is best, however, to interpret the phrase as a dative of means ("*by* the Spirit").[4] Arguments in favor of this position include the

1. This construction is not a simple dative but involves the preposition ἐν plus a dative. The use of a preposition to make the relationship more explicit was replacing the simple dative during the Koine period.
2. This is the preferred interpretation of most English versions as well as Clinton E. Arnold, *Ephesians*, ZECNT (Grand Rapids: Zondervan, 2010), 349–51; F. F. Bruce, *The Epistles to the Colossians, to Philemon, and to the Ephesians*, NICNT (Grand Rapids: Eerdmans, 1984), 379–80. Some even argue that both *content* and *means* are communicated in this verse: Markus Barth, *Ephesians 4–6*, AB 34A (Garden City, NY: Doubleday, 1974), 582; Andrew T. Lincoln, *Ephesians*, WBC (Dallas: Word, 1990), 344. Frank Thielman argues for a dative of sphere, "*in* the Spirit"; see *Ephesians*, BECNT (Grand Rapids: Baker Academic, 2010), 360.
3. See, e.g., Luke 2:40: πληρούμενον σοφίᾳ, "filled with wisdom"; Rom. 1:29: πεπληρωμένους πάσῃ ἀδικίᾳ, "They were filled with all manner of unrighteousness"; 2 Cor. 7:4: πεπλήρωμαι τῇ παρακλήσει, "I am filled with comfort." See also Ps. 65:4 (64:5 LXX); 3 Bar. 15.2; Sib. Or. 5.201; Let. Aris. 261.6; Herm. Mand. 5.2.7; 11.1.9; Ign. *Smyrn*. 1.1.
4. This is the preferred interpretation of the CSB and NET; Wallace 93, 170–71, 215, 375; Ernest Best, *Ephesians*, ICC (London: T&T Clark, 1998), 501, 508; Harold W. Hoehner, *Ephesians: An Exegetical Commentary* (Grand Rapids: Baker

following: (1) The *dative of means* is a "very common" category, whereas the *dative of content* is "extremely rare" (Wallace 162, 170). There are only three clear uses of this category in all the NT, and all three uses are simple datives: Luke 2:40; Romans 1:29; 2 Corinthians 7:4. (2) There are no other biblical examples of ἐν plus the dative following πληρόω expressing content. Normally the genitive would be used to convey this meaning.[5] (3) The parallel with οἴνῳ, which is clearly a dative of means ("Do not get drunk [by means of] wine"),[6] suggests the same usage here. (4) The parallel with Galatians 5:16, where Paul instructs his readers to "walk by the Spirit" (πνεύματι περιπατεῖτε) is consistent with this interpretation.

If ἐν πνεύματι represents the *means* of the filling (*"by* the Spirit"), then what is the *content* of the filling? This question must be answered by taking into consideration the entire Epistle of Ephesians, specifically Paul's use of "fullness" language. In 1:23 the church as the body of Christ participates in Christ's fullness. In 3:19 Paul prays that his readers would "be filled with all the fullness of God" (πληρωθῆτε εἰς πᾶν τὸ πλήρωμα τοῦ θεοῦ). In 4:10 Christ is said to have ascended so "that he might fill all things" (πληρώσῃ τὰ πάντα). In 4:13 the goal of believers' maturity is defined in terms of "the fullness of Christ" (τοῦ πληρώματος τοῦ Χριστοῦ). Thus, while the Spirit is the means by which believers are filled, the content of their filling is the fullness of the Triune God. Wallace (375) summarizes: "Believers are to be filled *by* Christ *by means of* the Spirit *with* the content of the fullness of God."

---

Academic, 2002), 704. Cf. Eph. 4:30, μὴ λυπεῖτε τὸ πνεῦμα τὸ ἅγιον τοῦ θεοῦ, ἐν ᾧ ἐσφραγίσθητε, "Do not grieve the Holy Spirit of God, by whom you were sealed." The dative relative pronoun (referring to the Holy Spirit) is a dative of means; cf. also Rom. 15:16; 1 Cor. 12:3.

5. See Luke 1:15 (πνεύματος ἁγίου πλησθήσεται), 41 (ἐπλήσθη πνεύματος ἁγίου), 67 (ἐπλήσθη πνεύματος ἁγίου); Acts 2:4 (ἐπλήσθησαν . . . πνεύματος ἁγίου), 28 (πληρώσεις . . . εὐφροσύνης); 4:8 (πλησθεὶς πνεύματος ἁγίου), 31 (ἐπλήσθησαν . . . τοῦ ἁγίου πνεύματος); 9:17 (πλησθῇς πνεύματος ἁγίου); 13:9 (πλησθεὶς πνεύματος ἁγίου), 52 (ἐπληροῦντο χαρᾶς καὶ πνεύματος ἁγίου); Rom. 15:13 (πληρώσαι . . . πάσης χαρᾶς καὶ εἰρήνης), 14 (πεπληρωμένοι πάσης [τῆς] γνώσεως).

6. So Robertson 533; Wallace 375.

# 7

# ACCUSATIVE CASE

## Romans 10:9

### Introduction

Romans 10:9 states, "If you confess with your mouth that Jesus is Lord and believe in your heart that God raised him from the dead, you will be saved." In fact, "everyone who calls on the name of the Lord will be saved" (Rom. 10:13). But what precisely is it that a person is to confess? Interestingly, various English translations render verse 9 differently.

- "Jesus is Lord" (CSB, ESV, NIV, NLT, NRSV, RSV)
- "Jesus as Lord" (NASB)
- "the Lord Jesus" (KJV, NKJV)

Why is this phrase translated in various ways, and what is the difference in meaning (if any)?

### Overview

The accusative case is considered the case of *limitation* since it often limits the action of a verb. More specifically, it can convey the end, direction, or extent of an action, often answering the question "how far?" (D&M 91–92). Wallace (178) helpfully explains the distinction between the accusative case and both the genitive and dative cases: "The *genitive* limits as to *quality* while the *accusative* limits as to *quantity*. . . . The dative is concerned about that to which the action of the verb is related, located, or by which it is accomplished, while the accusative is concerned about the extent and the scope of the verb's action."

- *Direct object* (indicates the recipient/object of the verbal action): "Preach the word [τὸν λόγον]" (2 Tim. 4:2).

- *Double accusative* (when a verb has more than one accusative object to complete the thought): "the Father has sent the Son to be the Savior [τὸν υἱὸν σωτῆρα]" (1 John 4:14 NASB).

- *Apposition* (provides additional information to a substantive in the accusative case): "Jesus Christ the Righteous One [δίκαιον]" (1 John 2:1 CSB).

- *Measure* (indicates the extent [regarding time or space] of a verbal action): "serving night and day [νύκτα καὶ ἡμέραν]" (Luke 2:37 NASB).

- *Manner* (specifies the manner in which a verbal action is performed): "Freely [δωρεάν] give" (Matt. 10:8 NASB).

- *Respect* (limits or qualifies the extent of the verbal action): "They were cut to the heart [τὴν καρδίαν]" (Acts 2:37).

- *Subject of infinitive* (functions as the subject of an infinitive, indicating the agent performing the action conveyed by the infinitive): "so that we [ἡμᾶς] . . . might be to the praise of his glory" (Eph. 1:12).

### Interpretation

In some contexts, a verb may take more than one object to complete the meaning. In this case, both direct objects are found in the accusative case. There are two types of double accusative constructions: (1) a personal and impersonal object (γάλα ὑμᾶς ἐπότισα, "I fed you milk," 1 Cor. 3:2 NET)[1] or (2) an object and complement (ὁ δοὺς ἑαυτὸν ἀντίλυτρον, "who gave himself as a ransom," 1 Tim. 2:6).[2] In the second example, the first accusative is the verbal object while the second accusative serves as the predicate complement.[3] Now to go back to our example (Rom. 10:9), must someone confess "Jesus is Lord," "Jesus as Lord," or "the Lord Jesus"? The verse reads, ὅτι ἐὰν ὁμολογήσῃς ἐν τῷ στόματί σου κύριον Ἰησοῦν. Here the verse presents a double accusative in an object-complement construction. The two accusatives are κύριον and Ἰησοῦν, with the proper name Ἰησοῦν serving as the object and κύριον functioning as the complement. Of the three translation options mentioned above, the last option ("the Lord Jesus") is the least likely, since one would expect the definite article before κύριον.[4] There does not seem to be a major distinction between the first two options ("Jesus is Lord" and "Jesus as Lord"), although the first option is best "because the object-complement construction is semantically equivalent to the subject-predicate nominative construction" (Wallace 184). Thus the phrase, although in the accusative, is essentially the same as someone stating "Jesus is Lord" (κύριος Ἰησοῦς).[5]

But we must be careful not to pass over this confession too quickly (cf. 2 Cor. 4:5). Dunn writes, "To confess someone as 'lord' denotes an attitude of subserviency and sense of belonging or devotion to the

---

1. Verbs often used with a double accusative person-impersonal construction include the following categories: verbs of (1) teaching (διδάσκω) and reminding (ἀναμιμνήσκω), (2) clothing (ἐκδύω) and anointing (χρίω), and (3) inquiring (ἐρωτάω) and asking (αἰτέω), and certain causative verbs (ποτίζω, φορτίζω). See Wallace 181–82.
2. Verbs often used with a double accusative object-complement construction include the following categories: (1) calling (καλέω), designating (λέγω), and confessing (ὁμολογέω), (2) making or appointing (ποιέω), (3) sending (ἀποστέλλω) and expelling (ἐκβάλλω), (4) considering (λογίζομαι, νομίζω) and regarding (ἡγέομαι), and (5) declaring or presenting (ἀποδείκνυμι, δίδωμι, παραδίδωμι, παρίστημι, προτίθημι). See Wallace 182–85.
3. Although the object is usually first, as we will see from Rom. 10:9, that is not always the case.
4. Cf. Acts 11:17, 20; 16:31; Rom. 13:14; 2 Cor. 4:14; Col. 2:6; Philem. 5.
5. Cf. the following subject-predicate nominative constructions: (1) 1 Cor. 12:3: "Therefore I want you to understand that no one speaking in the Spirit of God ever says 'Jesus is accursed!' [Ἀνάθεμα Ἰησοῦς] and no one can say 'Jesus is Lord' [Κύριος Ἰησοῦς] except in the Holy Spirit"; (2) Phil. 2:11: Paul writes that one day "every tongue [will] confess that Jesus Christ is Lord [κύριος Ἰησοῦς Χριστός]."

one so named. And if the confession here was used in baptism, . . . it would also indicate a transfer of allegiance, a change in acknowledged ownership. . . . The clear implication is that Jesus as Lord shares in the one God's lordship."[6] In addition, the confession that Jesus is Lord is a direct affront to the proclaimed lordship of the Roman emperor. As Michael Bird declares,

> A Christian is someone who professes to live under submission of King Jesus and believes that God has acted in Jesus to usher in the age to come. Not only that, what is provocative is that Paul writes these words to a cluster of house churches in the heart of the Roman Empire, living right under the emperor's nose and boldly declaring the lordship of a Jewish man executed by the Romans as a common criminal. It's provocative because the Roman emperor was the one hailed as *Kyrios* by supplicants and clients across the empire. . . . Whether Paul intends the statement "Jesus is Lord" to be heard as a deliberate sociopolitical protest against the propaganda of the imperial cult is debatable. But at least we should acknowledge that the claim was potentially incendiary and could be perceived as politically disloyal. To claim that "Jesus is Lord" on Lord Nero's own turf was not going to endear the Christians to imperial authorities.[7]

Thus, in order for someone to receive salvation, they must not only believe in their heart that God raised Jesus from the dead but also publicly declare the lordship of Jesus over their lives.

---

6. James D. G. Dunn, *Romans*, WBC 38B (Dallas: Word, 1988), 608.
7. Michael Bird, *Romans*, Story of God Bible Commentary (Grand Rapids: Zondervan, 2016), 359.

# 8

# THE ARTICLE

## 1 Timothy 3:2

### Introduction

Although the organizational structure of a local church may not be the *most* important issue, it certainly is an important issue. Other issues such as the truth of the gospel, the Trinity, justification by faith alone, and the substitutionary atonement of Christ are certainly more important. And yet, how one organizes a church is crucial because it often determines *who* can be a leader, *what* a leader does, and *what kind* of qualifications a leader must have. In 1 Timothy 3:1–7 Paul gives the necessary qualifications for someone who serves as an overseer. At the beginning of the list he writes, "Therefore an overseer [τὸν ἐπίσκοπον] must be above reproach" (v. 2). Interestingly, Paul includes the article before the title "overseer." Some have taken this to mean that Paul (or for many who argue this point, some later person writing under Paul's name) is referring to a single "overseer" or "bishop" who holds an office above the elders. But precisely how is the article functioning? Is the text indicating that a *single* overseer should lead each church as "the overseer," or is the text referring generically to anyone who might serve in such a capacity as "an overseer"?

## Overview

The article is the most frequent word in the NT, with nearly 20,000 occurrences. It is a small word (often only one letter) that can easily be missed and its presence (or absence) virtually unnoticed. And yet it is a word that is often significant to our understanding of Scripture. The article has at least three basic functions: (1) as substantiver the article can transform various parts of speech into virtual nouns; (2) as distinguisher the article can differentiate one substantive from another (or others); and (3) as definitizer the article can make a substantive definite. Below are some of the more specific uses of the article:

- *Identification* (the article identifies a particular individual, group, or object from another [or others], often turning various parts of speech into substantives): "Where is the one who has been born [ὁ τεχθείς] king of the Jews?" (Matt. 2:2 NIV).

- *Par excellence* (the article identifies someone who is alone in a class): "Are you the Prophet [ὁ προφήτης]?" (John 1:21).

- *Monadic* (the article identifies someone or something that is unique or one of a kind): "the kingdom [ἡ βασιλεία] of God is at hand" (Mark 1:15).

- *Previous reference / anaphoric* (the article points back to a substantive that was previously mentioned): "Where do you get that living water [τὸ ὕδωρ τὸ ζῶν]?" (John 4:11, referring back to the living water mentioned in v. 10).

- *With abstract nouns* (the article is often used with abstract nouns when such nouns would not use the definite article in English): "Love [ἡ ἀγάπη] is patient" (1 Cor. 13:4).

- *Generic* (the article identifies a group or class; e.g., "the man on the street"): "the worker [ὁ ἐργάτης] is worthy of his wages" (1 Tim. 5:18 CSB).

- *As a pronoun* (the article can function like the following pronouns: [1] personal, [2] possessive, [3] demonstrative, and [4] alternate): "But he [ὁ] said to them" (John 4:32).

## Interpretation

Does the presence of the article in 1 Timothy 3:2 (τὸν ἐπίσκοπον) indicate the elevation of one overseer above the elders?[1] This is the position of Campenhausen, who states, "In the Pastoral Epistles the 'bishop' is always spoken of in the singular. The simplest explanation of this fact is that monarchical episcopacy is by now the prevailing system, and that the one bishop has already become the head of the presbyterate."[2] Or is Paul merely indicating that any individual who is to serve as an overseer must meet the accompanying qualifications? In other words, is the use of the article monadic or generic? There are at least five reasons why the article should be viewed generically, thus indicating a representative from a particular class and not a singular officeholder.[3]

First, it is natural to use the generic singular, since every overseer must individually meet the qualifications. The singular form refers to anyone who would meet the qualifications listed. Thus Paul is not indicating that there is only one overseer in each church (or one bishop over a city); the singular indicates that overseers as a class are in view.

Second, the singular use of "the overseer" could have been influenced by the singular use of "if anyone" (εἴ τις) in the preceding verse (1 Tim. 3:1). Fee comments, "The 'if anyone' clause in verse 1, which has led to the singular in this verse, is a nonlimiting, or generalizing, conditional sentence. It recurs in 1 Timothy 5:8 and 6:3, and in both cases—esp. 6:3—refers to a group of more than one."[4]

1. The same question could also be raised concerning Titus 1:7.
2. Hans von Campenhausen, *Ecclesiastical Authority and Spiritual Power in the Church of the First Three Centuries*, trans. J. A. Baker (Stanford, CA: Stanford University Press, 1969), 107.
3. So Gordon Fee, *1 and 2 Timothy, Titus* (Grand Rapids: Baker, 1988), 84; Donald Guthrie, *The Pastoral Epistles*, rev. ed., TNTC 14 (Grand Rapids: Eerdmans, 1990), 32–33; J. N. D. Kelly, *A Commentary on the Pastoral Epistles*, BNTC (London: Adam & Charles Black, 1963), 13, 74; George W. Knight, *The Pastoral Epistles*, NIGTC (Grand Rapids: Eerdmans 1992), 155, 176; Thomas D. Lea and Hayne P. Griffin, *1, 2 Timothy, Titus*, NAC 34 (Nashville: Broadman, 1992), 109; I. Howard Marshall, *The Pastoral Epistles*, ICC (London: T&T Clark, 1999), 160, 178, 477; William D. Mounce, *Pastoral Epistles*, WBC 46 (Nashville: Nelson, 2000), 163; Phillip H. Towner, *Letters to Timothy and Titus*, NICNT (Grand Rapids: Eerdmans, 2006), 246–47, 686.
4. Fee, *1 and 2 Timothy, Titus*, 84. Mounce (*Pastoral Epistles*, 163) likewise comments: "In 1 Timothy it appears that since there is only one office of overseer (with

CHAPTER 8

Third, it is not uncommon for Paul to alternate between singular and plural generic nouns, particularly within the Pastoral Epistles. For example, in 1 Timothy 2:8 Paul addresses the *men* (τοὺς ἄνδρας) but then speaks of the singular *man* (ἀνδρός) in verse 12. In 1 Timothy 2:9 Paul exhorts the *women* (γυναῖκας) to adorn themselves in modest apparel, but in verse 11 he says, "Let a *woman* [γυνή] learn quietly with all submissiveness."[5] In 1 Timothy 2:15 Paul concludes his discussion on the role of women by stating, "*She* will be saved [σωθήσεται] through childbearing—if *they* continue [μείνωσιν] in faith and love and holiness, with self-control." In 1 Timothy 5:1 Paul commands Timothy not to rebuke an *older man* (πρεσβυτέρῳ) but to exhort him as a father (πατέρα) and the *younger men* (νεωτέρους) as brothers (ἀδελφούς). In verses 3 and 4 of the same chapter, Paul reminds the church to "honor *widows* [χήρας] who are truly widows" and then goes on to say, "But if a *widow* [χήρα] has children or grandchildren." In verse 11 he switches back to the plural when he speaks of the "younger widows" (νεωτέρας χήρας). Finally, 1 Timothy 5:17 states that "elders [πρεσβύτεροι] who rule well" are "worthy of double honor." Yet in verse 19 we are told that the church should "not receive an accusation against an elder [πρεσβυτέρου] except on the basis of two or three witnesses" (NASB). Verse 20 then speaks of "*those* who are sinning [τοὺς ἁμαρτάνοντας]" (NKJV), which most agree refers to the elders. Based on this pattern found in the Pastoral Epistles, one should not be surprised to find the author first referring to the "elders" (plural) and then to the "overseer" (singular).

Fourth, the pattern of NT leadership is that churches were led by a plurality of leaders. So, although the singular is used in 1 Timothy 3:2, the consistent testimony of the NT is that each congregation had a multiplicity of leaders instead of a single leader with unmatched authority. In fact, there is no example in the NT of one elder or pastor

---

many fulfilling the role), Paul begins 3:1–7 with the generic singular . . . and to stay consistent continues with singular forms." See 1 Tim. 5:8: "But if anyone [εἰ δέ τις] does not provide for his relatives, . . . he has denied the faith and is worse than an unbeliever"; 1 Tim. 6:3–4: "If anyone [εἴ τις] teaches a different doctrine, . . . he is puffed up with conceit and understands nothing."

5. Italics added here and in the subsequent verses in this paragraph.

leading a congregation as the sole or primary leader. There was a plurality of elders at the churches in Judea (Acts 11:30); Antioch of Pisidia, Lystra, Iconium, and Derbe (Acts 14:23); Ephesus (Acts 20:17; 1 Tim. 5:17); Philippi (Phil. 1:1); the towns of Crete (Titus 1:5); the churches in the dispersion to which James wrote (James 1:1); the Roman provinces of Pontus, Galatia, Cappadocia, Asia, and Bithynia (1 Pet. 5:1); and the church(es) to which Hebrews was written (Heb. 13:7, 17, 24).

Fifth, the terms "elder" and "overseer" are used interchangeably in the NT. This last point corresponds with the previous one because the term "overseer" (ἐπίσκοπος) is not used often in the NT. Thus the evidence garnered in the previous section is somewhat contingent on the terms ἐπίσκοπος and πρεσβύτερος being used interchangeably. In Acts 20 Paul sends for the elders (τοὺς πρεσβυτέρους) of Ephesus to exhort them in their work (20:17). He charges them to take heed to themselves and to all the flock since the Holy Spirit has made them "overseers" (ἐπισκόπους) to shepherd the church of God (20:28). Luke first records that Paul calls them elders, but then has Paul referring to them as overseers: "He sent to Ephesus and called for the elders of the church. . . . The Holy Spirit has made you overseers" (20:17, 28). Another example of the close connection between elder and overseer is found in 1 Peter 5:1–2, which states, "The elders [πρεσβυτέρους] who are among you I exhort: . . . Shepherd the flock of God which is among you, serving as overseers [ἐπισκοποῦντες]" (NKJV). Although the verb form is used (ἐπισκοπέω), this text demonstrates that the duties of an elder involve exercising oversight over the church.

Perhaps the most convincing passage demonstrating that the terms elder and overseer are interchangeable is Titus 1:5–7. In verse 5, Paul writes to Titus, "This is why I left you in Crete, so that you might put what remained into order, and appoint elders [πρεσβυτέρους] in every town as I directed you." When Paul gives the qualifications in verse 7, however, he replaces the term "elder" with "overseer." He continues, "For an overseer [τὸν ἐπίσκοπον], as God's steward, must be above reproach." Here, as in 1 Timothy 3:2, the singular form with the article is used. The previous reference to "elders" in Titus 1:5, however, demonstrates that a single bishop is not what Paul has in mind.[6] Therefore, in 1 Timothy 3:2, when Paul uses the singular ἐπίσκοπος with the article, the best option is to interpret the article as generic: each individual potential candidate must meet the various qualifications.

6. For a more thorough discussion of this topic, see Benjamin L. Merkle, *40 Questions about Elders and Deacons* (Grand Rapids: Kregel, 2008), 76–83.

# 9

# THE GRANVILLE
# SHARP RULE

## Titus 2:13

## Introduction

Does the NT really teach the full deity of Jesus Christ? Some scholars think this unlikely since all but one (Luke) of the NT authors were Jews, and to be Jewish is to firmly confess monotheism. Additionally, it is sometimes argued that the theology of the earliest Christians was somewhat undeveloped and therefore the concept of Jesus's deity is not clearly found in the NT. But here is where Greek grammar can help us correctly interpret some controversial passages of the NT. For example, in Titus 2:13 does Paul really call Jesus God when he states that as believers we are "waiting for our blessed hope, the appearing of the glory of our great God and Savior Jesus Christ"? The Granville Sharp rule will help us answer this question.

## Overview

The Granville Sharp rule states that when a single article governs two nouns (substantives) of the same case that are connected by καί, they refer to the same person. This rule applies only to nouns that are (1) singular, (2) personal, (3) nonproper, and (4) in the same case.[1] For example, Hebrews 3:1 states that Jesus is "the apostle and high priest of our confession" (τὸν ἀπόστολον καὶ ἀρχιερέα τῆς ὁμολογίας ἡμῶν). This construction makes clear that Jesus is both the *apostle* and the *high priest*. Conversely, 1 John 2:22 does not qualify because the two nouns are not governed by one article: "he who denies the Father and the Son" (ὁ ἀρνούμενος τὸν πατέρα καὶ τὸν υἱόν). Similarly, John 7:45 does not qualify because the nouns are plural and one is a proper name: "The officers then came to the chief priests and Pharisees" (ἦλθον οὖν οἱ ὑπηρέται πρὸς τοὺς ἀρχιερεῖς καὶ Φαρισαίους).

## Interpretation

There are three main views regarding the interpretation of Titus 2:13 in relation to the deity of Christ. The first view does not acknowledge that the Granville Sharp rule applies to this text. For example, the KJV states, "Looking for that blessed hope, and the glorious appearing of the great God and our Saviour Jesus Christ." Translated in this manner, "the great God" and "our Saviour Jesus Christ" denote two separate persons. This interpretation is not followed by modern English versions and has been rejected by most commentators.[2]

The second and third views both accept the validity of the Granville Sharp rule for Titus 2:13. Because the article τοῦ governs both θεοῦ and σωτῆρος with καί connecting the two nouns that are singular, personal, and nonproper,[3] they refer to the same person. Where these views differ is regarding the function of Ἰησοῦ Χριστοῦ. Is it in apposition to τῆς δόξης or to τοῦ μεγάλου θεοῦ καὶ σωτῆρος ἡμῶν? View 2 claims that it is in apposition to "glory" (τῆς δόξης) and so Paul is

---

1. The word *rule* may be stating too much, since this is merely a pattern that Sharp noticed.
2. Even the NKJV rejected this interpretation and reads, "looking for the blessed hope and glorious appearing of our great God and Savior Jesus Christ." This position is affirmed by J. N. D. Kelly, *A Commentary on the Pastoral Epistles*, BNTC (London: Adam & Charles Black, 1963), 246–47.
3. For the argument that θεός is not a proper name, see Wallace 272n42.

affirming that God's glory is seen in Jesus Christ but is not necessarily God himself. Hence the phrase τοῦ μεγάλου θεοῦ καὶ σωτῆρος ἡμῶν refers to God the Father and not specifically to Jesus Christ. View 3 (the traditional view) claims that Ἰησοῦ Χριστοῦ is in apposition to "our great God and Savior" (τοῦ μεγάλου θεοῦ καὶ σωτῆρος ἡμῶν). Thus Paul is affirming that such a person is none other than "Jesus Christ."

Although view 2 has several proponents who have made strong arguments,[4] there are several reasons why view 3 should be preferred.

1. The antecedent of a noun in an appositional construction typically directly precedes it, making it much more likely that Ἰησοῦ Χριστοῦ is in apposition to τοῦ μεγάλου θεοῦ καὶ σωτῆρος ἡμῶν and not τῆς δόξης.[5]

2. The term ἐπιφάνειαν (appearing) in Paul always refers to the first or second coming of Jesus and never to God (2 Thess. 2:8; 1 Tim. 6:14; 2 Tim. 1:9–10; 4:1, 8).

3. Elsewhere Paul never refers to Jesus as "the glory" of God, but he does call Jesus "Savior" (2 Tim. 1:10; Titus 1:4; 3:6).

4. In the next verse Paul links Jesus Christ to the concept of Savior by stating "who gave himself for us to redeem us" (Titus 2:14). Thus, in this context, it is Jesus Christ who is "our Savior."

4. See J. Christopher Edwards, "The Christology of Titus 2:13 and 1 Timothy 2:5," *TynBul* 62 (2011): 143–47; Gordon Fee, *1 and 2 Timothy, Titus* (Grand Rapids: Baker, 1988), 196; Phillip H. Towner, *Letters to Timothy and Titus*, NICNT (Grand Rapids: Eerdmans, 2006), 758. For a compelling response to Edwards, see Murray J. Harris, "A Brief Response to 'The Christology of Titus 2:13 and 1 Timothy 2:5' by J. Christopher Edwards," *TynBul* 62 (2011): 149–50. For a compelling response to Fee, see Robert M. Bowman Jr., "Jesus Christ, God Manifest: Titus 2:13 Revisited," *JETS* 51 (2008): 733–52.

5. George W. Knight notes that a major problem with view 2 is that "it requires an appositional reference that is quite far removed, and it is a solution that is certainly less obvious than the alternatives, or at least than [the traditional] interpretation." *The Pastoral Epistles*, NIGTC (Grand Rapids: Eerdmans, 1992), 325. Furthermore, if the genitive noun τῆς δόξης is taken as an attributive genitive modifying ἐπιφάνειαν ("appearing of glory" = "glorious appearing"), it would rule out the possibility of τῆς δόξης being in an appositional relationship. Most commentators seem to take τῆς δόξης as a subjective genitive. For a defense of the attributive genitive, see Bowman, "Jesus Christ, God Manifest," 733–52.

5. The phrase "God and Savior" was a common title in Jewish and Hellenistic religious discourse. Thus the terms are naturally linked together.

6. The adjective "great" (μέγας) is better explained as a designation of Christ since it is never used of God the Father in the NT (the greatness of God is assumed). Again, this may be used to contrast Jesus with the pagan deities of the various first-century religions.

7. It is not unprecedented to refer to Jesus as God.[6] In fact, a similar construction is used in 2 Peter 1:1, where Peter addresses his readers as those "who have obtained a faith of equal standing with ours by the righteousness of our God and Savior Jesus Christ" (τοῖς ἰσότιμον ἡμῖν λαχοῦσιν πίστιν ἐν δικαιοσύνῃ τοῦ θεοῦ ἡμῶν καὶ σωτῆρος Ἰησοῦ Χριστοῦ).

8. This is the interpretation of most grammarians and commentators and nearly all English Bible versions.[7]

We conclude with two quotations, one from a grammarian and one from a commentator:

6. Other NT passages that affirm the deity of Christ by ascribing to him the title of θεός include the following: John 1:1, "In the beginning was the Word, and the Word was with God, and the Word was God"; 1:18, "No one has ever seen God; the only God, who is at the Father's side, he has made him known"; 20:28, "Thomas answered him [i.e., Jesus], 'My Lord and my God!'"; Rom. 9:5, "To them belong the patriarchs, and from their race, according to the flesh, is the Christ, who is God over all, blessed forever. Amen"; Heb. 1:8, "But of the Son he says, 'Your throne, O God, is forever and ever, the scepter of uprightness is the scepter of your kingdom'"; 1 John 5:20, "And we know that the Son of God has come and has given us understanding, so that we may know him who is true; and we are in him who is true, in his Son Jesus Christ. He is the true God and eternal life."

7. Grammars: BDF §276.3, p. 145; B&W 76; D&M 147; C. F. D. Moule, *An Idiom Book of New Testament Greek* (Cambridge: Cambridge University Press, 1953), 109–10; Robertson 786; Wallace 276, 290; Young 63; Zerwick, *Bib. Gk.*, §185, p. 60 (tentatively).

Commentators: Donald Guthrie, *The Pastoral Epistles*, rev. ed., TNTC 14 (Grand Rapids: Eerdmans, 1990), 212; Knight, *Pastoral Epistles*, 322–26; Andreas J. Köstenberger, *1–2 Timothy and Titus*, BTCP (Nashville: B&H, 2017), 339–40; Jerome D. Quinn, *The Letter to Titus*, AB 35 (New York: Doubleday, 1990), 155–56; I. Howard Marshall, *The Pastoral Epistles*, ICC (London: T&T Clark, 1999), 276–82; William D. Mounce, *Pastoral Epistles*, WBC 46 (Nashville: Nelson, 2000), 426–31. See also Murray J. Harris, Theos *in Reference to Jesus* (Grand Rapids: Baker, 1992), 173–85, 301–13.

Bible versions: CSB, ESV, NASB, NIV, NKJV, NLT, NRSV, and others.

A proper understanding of the [Granville Sharp] rule shows it to have the highest degree of validity with the NT. Consequently, these two passages [i.e., Titus 2:13 and 2 Pet. 1:1] are as secure as any in the canon when it comes to identifying Christ as θεός. (Wallace 290)

A Christological pronouncement on the divinity of Christ . . . is the most natural reading of the text [i.e., Titus 2:13], is required by the grammar, concurs with Paul's use of ἐπιφάνεια, "appearing," accounts for the singular use of the phrase "God and savior" in secular thought, and fits the context well. (Mounce, *Pastoral Epistles*, 431)

# 10

# COLWELL'S CANON

## 1 Timothy 6:10

### Introduction

We all know that *things* in themselves are not sinful. But they can be if they are viewed or used inappropriately. In 1 Timothy 6:10 Paul warns his protégé Timothy: "For the love of money is a root of all kinds of evil," ῥίζα γὰρ πάντων τῶν κακῶν ἐστιν ἡ φιλαργυρία (CSB). The King James Version, however, reads, "For the love of money is the root of all evil." So, is the love of money *a* root or *the* root of evil? And is it the root of *all kinds* of evil or of *all* evil?

### Overview

Colwell's Canon (or Rule) states that a *definite* predicate nominative does not usually take the article when preceding a copulative (linking) verb. Or, as Colwell put it, "A definite predicate nominative has the article when it follows the verb, [but] it does not have the article when it precedes the verb."[1] In other words, an anarthrous (i.e., having no

---

1. E. C. Colwell, "A Definite Rule for the Use of the Article in the Greek New Testament," *JBL* 52 (1933): 13. This is a pattern and not a strict "rule," since there are exceptions. For example, Colwell (17) notes that 90 percent of definite

article) predicate nominative can be definite because this grammatical rule states that the location of the predicate nominative (whether it precedes or follows the copulative verb, usually εἰμί or γίνομαι) dictates whether the article is included or not. Thus, if the predicate nominative *follows* the copulative verb, then the article is included: Ἐγώ εἰμι τὸ φῶς τοῦ κόσμου, "I am the light of the world" (John 8:12). But if the predicate nominative *precedes* the copulative verb, then the article is not included: φῶς εἰμι τοῦ κόσμου, "I am the light of the world" (John 9:5). In such cases, the *context* must determine whether the predicate nominative is definite.

## Interpretation

So does Paul mean that the love of money is *a* root or *the* root of evil (1 Tim. 6:10)? Let's analyze the sentence more closely: ῥίζα γὰρ πάντων τῶν κακῶν ἐστιν ἡ φιλαργυρία. The nominative *subject* of the sentence is "the love of money" (ἡ φιλαργυρία), and the *predicate* nominative is "root" (ῥίζα). Thus, because ῥίζα *precedes* the copulative verb (ἐστίν), the article is not included. Again, we must stress that the grammar requires this omission. The lack of an article has nothing to do with whether the noun is definite or not. Many English versions (e.g., CSB, ESV, NASB, NIV, NKJV, NRSV) render the noun as indefinite ("a root") presumably because it is difficult to maintain that the love of money is *the* root of all evil. The love of money might be *a* major factor that leads people to evil but it is not the only factor. Other versions (e.g., KJV, NET, NJB, NLT, RSV), however, render the noun as definite ("the root").

Another feature to consider is the meaning of πάντων τῶν κακῶν. Is this phrase best rendered "all kinds/sorts of evil" (CSB, ESV, NASB, NIV, NKJV, NLT, NRSV) or "all evil(s)" (KJV, NET, NJB, RSV)? Again, the theological issue at stake is whether it is indeed true that the love of money is a/the root of *all* evil. Certainly, πᾶς (all) can be used in some contexts to convey *all without distinction* ("all kinds")

---

predicate nominatives that have the article follow the verb, and 87 percent of definite predicate nominatives that do not have the article precede the verb. Of course, all of these stats assume that one's subjective categorization of definite or indefinite nouns is correct.

and does not necessarily convey *all without exception* ("all evil"). So which reading is correct?

Theologically it seems clear that the love of money is not the root or source of *all* evil. There is, however, another factor that must be considered. In the *context* Paul warns Timothy and the church at Ephesus to beware of the false teachers who love money. In contrast Paul reminds his readers that "godliness with contentment is great gain" (1 Tim. 6:6 CSB). He continues by warning them that "those who want to be rich fall into temptation, a trap, and many foolish and harmful desires, which plunge people into ruin and destruction" (1 Tim. 6:9 CSB). Paul then quotes a *proverb* to support his point: "The love of money is the root of all evil" (KJV). Thus, because Paul is citing a proverb, it should be translated as such. In other words, by their very nature, proverbs are *general truths* even though they are usually conveyed in absolute terms. For example, in Matthew 26:52 we read, "All [πάντες] who take up the sword will perish by the sword" (CSB). Yet, some might want to argue that Jesus is incorrect because surely not *all* who take up a sword are killed by a sword (or in battle). Certainly some soldiers were decommissioned from the army and lived many years in retirement. Because Jesus uttered a proverb, we know that pressing the meaning in an overly literal manner is inappropriate. It would simply not sound proverbial if Jesus stated, "*Many* who take up a sword will perish by a sword," even though that is the intended meaning.

Therefore, to interpret a proverb as an absolute truth is to misinterpret the intention of the author. Proverbs convey general truths but often use absolute or hyperbolic language to do so. Fee rightly comments, "It is the nature of proverbs to be brief, particular expressions of a truth, often imprecise, and for effect, often overstated."[2] Unfortunately, some commentators state that the lack of article favors "a root." Such an interpretation, however, fails to grasp the significance of Colwell's Canon. For example, Kelly maintains that the translation of "the root" is unwarranted since "there is no definite

---

2. Gordon D. Fee, *1 & 2 Timothy, Titus* (Grand Rapids: Baker, 1988), 145. See also Philip H. Towner, *The Letters to Timothy and Titus*, NICNT (Grand Rapids: Eerdmans, 2006), 403–4; I. H. Marshall, *The Pastoral Epistles*, ICC (London: T&T Clark, 1999), 651.

article before 'root' in the original Greek." He adds, "It is extravagant to assert that love of money is the root-cause of all sins."[3]

Because 1 Timothy 6:10 is a proverb, it is preferable to translate the Greek accordingly. "The love of money is the root of all evil" does not mean that the love of money is actually the root of *all* evil. It means that the person who is wise will understand that the love of money has led many people away from God down the path of evil. The English versions (and commentators) that fail to translate the statement as a proverb governed by Colwell's Canon do not do justice to the statement. As Towner declares, "To tame the translation is to soften the indictment of the greedy opponents" (*Letters to Timothy and Titus*, 404).

---

3. J. N. D. Kelly, *The Pastoral Epistles*, BNTC (London: Adam & Charles Black, 1963), 138. See also William D. Mounce, *Pastoral Epistles*, WBC 46 (Nashville: Thomas Nelson, 2000), 346; George W. Knight, *The Pastoral Epistles*, NIGTC (Grand Rapids: Eerdmans, 1992), 257.

# 11

# ADJECTIVES

## 2 Timothy 3:16

### Introduction

Perhaps the most significant verse related to the inspiration and authority of Scripture is 2 Timothy 3:16: "All Scripture is inspired by God and is profitable for teaching, for rebuking, for correcting, for training in righteousness" (CSB; πᾶσα γραφὴ θεόπνευστος καὶ ὠφέλιμος πρὸς διδασκαλίαν, πρὸς ἐλεγμόν, πρὸς ἐπανόρθωσιν, πρὸς παιδείαν τὴν ἐν δικαιοσύνῃ). But some have argued that the passage should be translated, "All Scripture inspired by God is profitable. . . ."[1] But what is the precise function of θεόπνευστος ("inspired by God" or, better, "God-breathed")? Does it function as a predicate adjective ("All Scripture is θεόπνευστος") or as an attributive adjective ("All θεόπνευστος Scripture is . . .")? Which translation is more likely, and what difference does it make?

---

1. See, e.g., Tyndale's translation: "For all Scripture given by inspiration of God is profitable. . . ." (archaic spelling updated).

## Overview

An adjective typically qualifies or describes a noun (or another substantive), distinguishing it from other nouns. In Greek, the adjective must agree with the nouns that it modifies in gender, case, and number. There are two basic uses of the adjective: (1) the general use and (2) that which conveys degree.

The general use has four main categories: (1) predicate, (2) attributive, (3) substantival, or (4) adverbial. With the predicate use, the adjective is used in conjunction with a copulative verb (such as εἰμί or γίνομαι, stated or implied), and the article will never directly precede the adjective. In other words, if the adjective is immediately preceded by the article, it cannot be the predicate use. With the attributive use, the adjective modifies an expressed noun. Three typical constructions are article-adjective-noun, article-noun-article-adjective, and noun-article-adjective. A substantival adjective functions similarly to a noun. Finally, the adverbial adjective modifies a verb instead of a noun (thus functioning like an adverb).

- *Predicate* (predicates a quality to the subject, with a copulative verb stated or implied): "But the Lord is faithful [πιστὸς δέ ἐστιν ὁ κύριος]" (2 Thess. 3:3).
- *Attributive* (ascribes a certain quality to a noun or substantive): "the good shepherd [ὁ ποιμὴν ὁ καλός]" (John 10:11).
- *Substantival* (functions as a noun in a given phrase): "to . . . the beloved [people] of God [ἀγαπητοῖς θεοῦ]" (Rom. 1:7 NABRE).
- *Adverbial* (modifies a verb rather than a noun): "But seek first [πρῶτον] the kingdom of God" (Matt. 6:33).

The use of the adjective that conveys degree also has four main categories (1) positive, (2) comparative, (3) superlative, and (4) elative. The positive adjective identifies the properties of a noun in relation to kind and not degree: "the rich man." The comparative adjective compares two persons or objects, specifying which is higher in degree in relation to the other: "the richer man." Two ways of forming a comparative adjective are (a) a third declension ending on a comparative noun (e.g., μείζων, "greater") or (b) adding -τερος to a positive degree adjective (e.g., πρέσβυς, "old" → πρεσβύτερος, "older"). These adjectives are often followed by a genitive of comparison or the particle ἤ (than). The superlative adjective involves a comparison of three or more entities: "the richest man." Two ways of forming a superlative are (a) adding -ιστος to a positive degree adjective (e.g., μέγας, "great" → μέγιστος, "greatest") or (b) adding -τατος to a positive degree adjective (e.g., ἅγιος, "holy" → ἁγιώτατος, "holiest"). Finally, the elative adjective involves a comparative or superlative adjective that does not necessarily make a comparison but intensifies the meaning, often translated with "very": "the very rich man."

- *Positive* (describes the properties of a noun in terms of kind rather than degree): "of the great [τῆς μεγάλης] city" (Rev. 11:8).

- *Comparative* (compares two entities by specifying which is higher in degree): "God is greater [μείζων] than our heart" (1 John 3:20).

- *Superlative* (compares three or more entities and indicates which is the highest in degree): "For I am the least [ὁ ἐλάχιστος] of the apostles" (1 Cor. 15:9).

- *Elative* (uses a comparative or superlative adjective to intensify the positive notion): "He has granted to us his precious and very great [μέγιστα] promises" (2 Pet. 1:4).

## Interpretation

The adjective θεόπνευστος occurs only in 2 Timothy 3:16 in the NT and is not found in the Septuagint. Most commentators agree that the term has a passive sense (i.e., that Scripture is the result of the breath of God) and not an active sense (i.e., that Scripture is filled with the breath of God). But exactly how is θεόπνευστος functioning in this verse? As a predicate adjective or as an attributive adjective?

Several factors can be listed in favor of interpreting θεόπνευστος as an attributive adjective: "All God-breathed Scripture is also profitable."

1. This option is grammatically possible and should not be dismissed without due consideration.

2. In constructions of πᾶς with a noun and adjective in the NT, the adjective is typically attributive (e.g., πᾶν ἔργον ἀγαθόν, "every good work," 2 Tim. 3:17).[2]

3. This usage would make πᾶσα γραφή parallel with ἱερὰ γράμματα ("sacred writings," 2 Tim. 3:15).

The majority of the evidence, however, favors interpreting θεόπνευστος as a predicate adjective.

1. The attributive view would require that καί be taken with an ascensive meaning ("all God-breathed Scripture is *also* profitable"), which is less likely since it seems to connect two adjectives ("all Scripture is God-breathed *and* profitable").[3] A similar construction found in 1 Timothy 4:4 (πᾶν κτίσμα θεοῦ καλὸν καὶ οὐδὲν ἀπόβλητον μετὰ εὐχαριστίας λαμβανόμενον, "everything created by God is good, *and* nothing is to be rejected if it is received with thanksgiving"), which is also interpreted as a predicate adjective. Wallace (313–14) summarizes: "The fact that καί means 'and' twelve times as often as it means 'also,' as well as the fact that it is unnatural to translate it adverbially as 'also' between two adjectives in the same case, argues for a predicate θεόπνευστος."

2. Some could argue that the attributive usage implies "that Paul did not regard all γραφή as God-breathed," which is not likely "since by γραφή he always means scripture" (Knight, *Pastoral Epistles*, 447).

3. In both Classical and Koine Greek (including the LXX and NT), the typical pattern for the adjective-noun-adjective construction

---

2. See also Matt. 7:17; 12:36; Acts 23:1; 2 Cor. 9:8; Eph. 1:3; 4:29; Col. 1:10; 2 Thess. 2:17; 2 Tim. 2:21; 4:18; Titus 1:16; 2:10; 3:1; Heb. 4:12; James 1:17; 3:16; Rev. 8:7; 18:2, 12; 21:19.

3. George W. Knight states, "The natural understanding of two adjectives connected by καί is that they are used in the same way, whether attributively or predicatively." *The Pastoral Epistles*, NIGTC (Grand Rapids: Eerdmans, 1992), 447; see also William D. Mounce, *Pastoral Epistles*, WBC 46 (Nashville: Nelson, 2000), 569.

(e.g., πᾶς-γραφή-θεόπνευστος) *in an equative clause* (i.e., a clause describing some feature of its subject) is that the first adjective is attributive ("*all* Scripture") and the second is predicate ("Scripture is *God-breathed*").[4]

Thus Paul declares that all of the Bible is sacred Scripture because of its divine source and is therefore profitable. In the original context, "Scripture" (γραφή) refers primarily to the OT but it also possibly includes the oral/written gospel message (cf. 1 Tim. 5:18; see, e.g., Mounce, *Pastoral Epistles*, 568). Most important, Paul indicates that it is the divine nature of Scripture that makes it so beneficial in producing individuals who are spiritually mature. This verse, then, gives Christians confidence that the Bible (God's inspired word) is the tool through which believers grow and mature in their faith. A few verses later Paul urges Timothy to "preach the word" (2 Tim. 4:2) because it is the word of God that has the power to transform the heart and mind. This should give us confidence to do the same.

---

4. Wallace (314) goes as far as calling this a "rule" when the first adjective is πᾶς: "In πᾶς + noun + adjective constructions in equative clauses the πᾶς, being by nature as definite as the article, implies the article, thus making the adjective(s) following the noun outside the implied article-noun group and, therefore, predicate."

# 12

# VERBAL ASPECT

## Matthew 16:24

## Introduction

One of Jesus's most well-known—but difficult—statements is found in Matthew 16:24: "If anyone would come after me, let him deny [ἀπαρνησάσθω] himself and take up [ἀράτω] his cross and follow [ἀκολουθείτω] me." Notice that in this verse we find two aorist imperatives (ἀπαρνησάσθω and ἀράτω) and one present imperative (ἀκολουθείτω). Why is there a shift in tense-forms (aspect), and how should they be interpreted?

## Overview

Simply stated, verbal aspect is the *viewpoint* or *perspective* by which an author chooses to portray an action (or state). That is, an author can present an action as (1) in process or ongoing (imperfective aspect = present or imperfect tense-form), (2) complete or as a whole (perfective aspect = aorist tense-form), or (3) a state of affairs resulting from a previous action (stative aspect = perfect tense-form). Because *time* is not communicated by the grammatical form of the verb outside of the indicative mood, aspect is primary. Thus, regardless of how the action actually happened, the author may choose to portray the action as in progress, as a whole, or as completed and with a resulting state.[1]

## Interpretation

So what are we to make of the change in tense-forms in Matthew 16:24? Before the modern understanding of verbal aspect, many grammarians and commentators believed that the tense-form conveys the *type* or *kind* of action performed. Thus they argued that the present tense-form means that the action is continuous, whereas the aorist tense-form conveys a once-and-for-all action. But scholars now recognize that the grammar of the verb (i.e., the tense-form) does not communicate such information. If a verb does convey such an action, it is based on other factors, such as the lexical meaning of the verb, the literary genre, or certain markers in the surrounding context.

Therefore, in Matthew 16:24, to argue that the switch in tense-forms signals a deliberate shift in the type of action required—from a once-and-for-all action to a continuous type of action—is probably unfounded. In other words, we are not on firm ground to argue from the verb tense-forms that Jesus is teaching that we must decisively come to the point where we deny ourselves and take up our cross and then keep following Jesus (continuous discipleship). For example, R. T. France comments, "The first two imperatives in this verse are aorist, and the last present, so that it may be inferred that 'denying oneself' and 'taking up the cross' are single, initiatory acts, to be followed by a continuing life of 'following.'"[2] But basing such

---

1. See Constantine R. Campbell, *Basics of Verbal Aspect in Biblical Greek* (Grand Rapids: Zondervan, 2008), 6; Buist M. Fanning, *Verbal Aspect in New Testament Greek* (Oxford: Clarendon, 1990), 84; K. L. McKay, *A New Syntax of the Verb in New Testament Greek: An Aspectual Approach*, SBG 5 (New York: Peter Lang, 1994), 27; Porter, *Idioms*, 21.

2. R. T. France, *The Gospel of Matthew*, NICNT (Grand Rapids: Eerdmans, 2007), 638. He wisely follows up this statement with "though this may be to press the usage of tenses too far." See also Grant R. Osborne, *Matthew*, ZECNT (Grand Rapids: Zondervan, 2010), 637; Robert H. Stein, *Mark*, BECNT (Grand Rapids: Baker Academic, 2008), 407.

a conclusion on the tense-form of the verbs is saying too much, since the tense-forms do not communicate the type of action.

More recently, however, some scholars have put too much weight on the tense-form (aspect) for different reasons.[3] For example, Porter notes that "the use of the imperfective aspect [i.e., the present tense-form of ἀκολουθείτω] *draws attention* to the process of going and following Jesus."[4] We must be careful not to attach too much significance to the subjective choice of the author, especially with the use of imperatives. I offer three reasons why we must resist the urge to overinterpret the switch in tense-forms.

First, some verbs, based on their lexical meaning, prefer one tense-form over another. For example, verbs that have a natural terminus (i.e., a natural end point) prefer the aorist tense-form, whereas those that have no natural terminus (i.e., no natural end point) or convey a state prefer the present tense-form. In this case, the verbs ἀπαρνέομαι (deny) and αἴρω (take up) convey actions that have a natural terminus (it doesn't take long to *deny* or *take up* something) and so prefer the aorist tense-form. This conclusion is confirmed by the actual usage of these verbs as imperatives: ἀπαρνέομαι occurs twice as an aorist imperative and never as a present imperative, and αἴρω occurs twenty-two times as an aorist imperative and only four times as a present imperative. In contrast, verbs of motion occur almost exclusively in the present tense-form in the imperative mood. For instance, ἀκολουθέω occurs sixteen times as a present imperative and only twice as an aorist imperative. Thus one would expect the present tense of ἀκολουθέω as the default imperatival form. If such is the case, then a subjective choice was not really made, since the form used is the conventional, default form. Consequently, it is problematic to argue that the author is drawing attention to the verb.

A second reason we should not press the differentiation between these tense-forms is that a distinction between the present tense-form as a continuous action and the aorist tense-form as a once-and-for-all action cannot be sustained. For example, in Acts 12:8 the present

3. See Benjamin L. Merkle, "The Abused Aspect: Neglecting the Influence of a Verb's Lexical Meaning on Tense-Form Choice," *BBR* 26, no. 1 (2016): 57–74.
4. Stanley E. Porter, *Verbal Aspect in the Greek of the New Testament, with Reference to Tense and Mood*, SBG 1 (New York: Peter Lang, 1989), 355, emphasis added.

tense-form of ἀκολουθέω is used for a onetime action and not for an ongoing action: "'Get dressed,' the angel told him, 'and put on your sandals.' And he did so. 'Wrap your cloak around you,' he told him, 'and follow [ἀκολούθει] me'" (CSB). This command given by the angel is obviously not a general (continuous) command but is a command for a specific (onetime) occasion.

Finally, although it is true that followers of Jesus must make a decisive, life-altering decision in their lives to repent of their sins and believe that Jesus is the Messiah, it is questionable that this is what Jesus is emphasizing. Is it not also true that followers of Jesus must make a daily decision to deny themselves and daily take up their crosses? In fact, this emphasis is brought out in Luke's Gospel, which adds that Christians must take up their cross "daily" (καθ' ἡμέραν, Luke 9:23). So, although Luke indicates that taking up one's cross is to be a repeated, daily act, the aorist tense-form is still used because of the lexical meaning of the verb. To claim that Jesus's commands in Matthew 16:24 (or Mark 8:34 or Luke 9:23) to deny oneself and to take up one's cross are each calling for a onetime act is pressing the imperatives too far. In fact, it can be argued, Jesus is teaching that denying oneself and taking up one's cross should also be an ongoing characteristic of his disciples.

# 13

# PRESENT INDICATIVES

1 John 3:6

## Introduction

It is easy to read our theology into a text. Of course, it is impossible to read the Bible without any presuppositions. But we should desire to read the text in such a way that we allow it to influence (and even correct) our theological system. We also need to be aware of, if possible, the original context so that we first attempt to interpret a passage in light of the original audience. In 1 John 3:6, the aged apostle John makes an amazing statement: "Everyone who remains in him does not sin [οὐχ ἁμαρτάνει]; everyone who sins [ὁ ἁμαρτάνων] has not seen him nor has known him" (trans. author). Is this text stating that (1) true Christians don't sin, (2) true Christians can get to the point where they are (at least temporarily) able not to sin, (3) true Christians are viewed eschatologically as sinless because of Christ's atoning work on the cross, or (4) true Christians don't continually or habitually sin?

## Overview

Although most present-tense indicative verbs refer to an action in the present time, it is also possible for present indicative verbs to convey an action that is past (e.g., historical present), future, or omnitemporal (e.g., gnomic). The aspect of present tense-form verbs is imperfective, meaning that the action is portrayed as progressive, internal, or incomplete.[1] The aspect and time also function together with lexical, grammatical, and contextual features to produce a wide variety of uses of the present tense in the indicative mood. Here is a list of the main uses of the present tense indicative:

- *Progressive* (an action ongoing or in progress): "The darkness is passing away [παράγεται]" (1 John 2:8).

- *Durative* (an action that began in the past and continues into the present): "For three years now I have come [ἔρχομαι]" (Luke 13:7).

- *Iterative* (an action performed repeatedly, regularly, or customarily): "You are always resisting [ἀντιπίπτετε] the Holy Spirit" (Acts 7:51 CSB).

- *Gnomic* (a statement that is timeless, universal, or generally true): "Every good tree produces [ποιεῖ] good fruit" (Matt. 7:17 CSB).

- *Instantaneous* (an action done immediately, usually by the very fact that it is spoken): "Father, I thank [εὐχαριστῶ] you" (John 11:41).

- *Historical* (a past event that adds vividness or gives literary prominence to some aspect of the story): "And a leper came [ἔρχεται] to him" (Mark 1:40).

- *Futuristic* (an action that will occur in the future): "Behold, he is coming [ἔρχεται] with the clouds" (Rev. 1:7).

## Interpretation

The Greek of 1 John 3:6 declares: πᾶς ὁ ἐν αὐτῷ μένων οὐχ ἁμαρτάνει· πᾶς ὁ ἁμαρτάνων οὐχ ἑώρακεν αὐτὸν οὐδὲ ἔγνωκεν αὐτόν. The center of most of the controversy regarding this verse revolves around the

---

1. *Internal* here means that the action is viewed from within the event rather than in terms of its beginning or end. See Wallace 514.

present tense-form verb ἁμαρτάνει. Of the four views given above, the first two are the most unlikely. The first view interprets the verse as claiming that true Christians don't sin. This understanding, however, contradicts both experience and other passages of Scripture. In fact, John himself previously stated, "If we say we have no sin, we deceive ourselves, and the truth is not in us" (1 John 1:8; see also 1:10; 2:1; 5:16). Additionally, this view is not easily compatible with the repeated injunctions to forsake sin and live righteously. The second view, though slightly better, is still unlikely since even the greatest saints struggle with sin until the end (e.g., King David and the apostle Peter).

So, is 1 John 3:6 declaring that eschatologically, from God's future perspective, Christians don't sin in light of the finished work of Christ (view 3)? This is the view of Daniel Wallace (525), who maintains that the immediate context is "speaking in terms of a projected eschatological reality" and is offering "a proleptic view of sanctification," that is, "a hyperbolic picture of believers, . . . implying that even though believers are not yet perfect, they are moving in that direction." Consequently "the author states in an absolute manner truths that are not yet true, because he is speaking within the context of eschatological hope" (Wallace 525). This interpretation views the present tense-form as gnomic; that is, as presenting a general truth about Christians. Thus even though Christians sin experientially, they don't sin positionally because of Christ's payment for sins on the cross.

The fourth view, however, is the most likely.[2] In 1 John 3:6 the verb ἁμαρτάνει should be interpreted as an iterative present, which involves the idea of a repetitive or customary action. This interpretation is expressed in both the ESV ("No one who abides in him keeps on sinning") and the NIV ("No one who lives in him keeps on sinning").[3] Several contextual factors indicate that ἁμαρτάνει should be interpreted as an iterative present. First, as we have already seen, John states that if we claim to be without sin, we deceive ourselves.

2. So Daniel L. Akin, 1, 2, 3 John, NAC 38 (Nashville: Broadman & Holman, 2001), 143.
3. See also NLT: "Anyone who continues to live in him will not sin. But anyone who keeps on sinning does not know him or understand who he is."

Thus John already implicitly acknowledges that perfection in this life is impossible (ruling out views 1 and 2). Second, the idea that John is speaking in light of our eschatological hope does not best fit the context of the letter. In this epistle, John offers a series of three repeated tests that serve to give assurance to true believers and expose false believers. The false believers are those who embrace an ungodly lifestyle, neglect to love others, and consequently continue to live in sin. Thus John is seeking to contrast the lifestyle of the false teachers with those who are genuine Christians.

Third, the iterative nuance is supported by the immediate context, where John has been repeatedly emphasizing the idea of *practicing* sin as a lifestyle:

- "everyone who practices sin" (πᾶς ὁ ποιῶν τὴν ἁμαρτίαν, 1 John 3:4 NASB).
- "the one who practices sin" (ὁ ποιῶν τὴν ἁμαρτίαν, 3:8 NASB).
- "No one who is born of God practices sin" (πᾶς ὁ γεγεννημένος ἐκ τοῦ θεοῦ ἁμαρτίαν οὐ ποιεῖ, 3:9 NASB).[4]

In the context, John has not only been referring to those who sin but specifically to those who practice or make a practice of sinning (using the verb ποιέω plus the noun ἁμαρτία). Thus John is not making a statement about the possibility of Christian perfectionism in this life or about our eschatological hope based on what Christ has done for us but is giving guidelines for recognizing the true children of God: those who are not characterized by habitual disobedience to God.

Finally, the use of the infinitive ἁμαρτάνειν in 3:9 helps confirm this interpretation. John adds that every believer "<u>cannot keep on sinning</u> [οὐ δύναται ἁμαρτάνειν], because he has been born of God." The construction δύναμαι + infinitive occurs 174 times in the NT, with the infinitive appearing 126 times in the aorist but only 48 times in the present. Thus δύναμαι tends to favor the aorist when in construction

---

4. See also John 8:34: "Jesus answered them, 'Truly, truly, I say to you, <u>everyone who practices sin</u> [πᾶς ὁ ποιῶν τὴν ἁμαρτίαν] is a slave to sin.'"

with an infinitive.[5] Based on this data, Baugh comments, "John consciously chose the present infinitive form ἁμαρτάνειν because he wished to convey a special nuance. That nuance is the 'characteristic' nature of the action, a lifestyle of sinning."[6] So not only does this interpretation fit the historical and literary contexts of 1 John, but the grammatical evidence also points in its favor.

5. Cf. μέλλω + infinitive (84 present; 7 aorist) and ἄρχομαι + infinitive (87 present; 0 aorist).
6. S. M. Baugh, *A First John Reader: Intermediate Greek Reading Notes and Grammar* (Phillipsburg, NJ: P&R, 1999), 52.

# 14

# IMPERFECT
# INDICATIVES

## Galatians 1:13

### Introduction

Before the apostle Paul's Damascus road experience, he wholeheartedly fought against Christians. When Stephen was martyred, we read, "And Saul approved of his execution" (Acts 8:1). Indeed, "Saul was ravaging the church, and entering house after house, he dragged off men and women and committed them to prison" (8:3). Not being content with his efforts and "still breathing threats and murder against the disciples of the Lord," Saul "went to the high priest and asked him for letters to the synagogues at Damascus, so that if he found any belonging to the Way, men or women, he might bring them bound to Jerusalem" (Acts 9:1–2). After Paul accepted Jesus as the promised Messiah, other believers were slow to embrace him as a true follower of the Way because of his previous actions.

But Paul did not forget his past. Rather, he often used it as an example of the grace of God. Writing to Timothy and to the church at Ephesus, he reminds them of his past by saying, "I was formerly a blasphemer and a persecutor and a violent aggressor. Yet I was shown mercy because I acted ignorantly in unbelief" (1 Tim. 1:13 NASB). When explaining his apostolic authority earlier to the Galatians, he reminds them of how they heard of Paul's earlier exploits in Judaism. He admits, "I persecuted the church of God violently and tried to destroy it" (Gal. 1:13). Later he adds that after his conversion, some were hearing, "He who used to persecute us is now preaching the faith he once tried to destroy" (1:23). Twice in Galatians the text states that Paul "was destroying" (ἐπόρθουν, imperfect) the church. And yet, nearly every translation adds the words "trying to," as in "I/he was trying to destroy." Is this a legitimate addition, or is it the intrusion of theology into the text?

## Overview

Like the present tense-form, the imperfect tense-form carries the same aspectual significance (imperfective aspect), portraying the action as progressive, internal, or incomplete.[1] Because it does not occur outside of the indicative mood, the time of the imperfect is almost always past time (which is conveyed by the presence of the augment). The categories below are essentially the same as those found with the present tense-form. This overlap is due to their aspectual similarity. It must be remembered that the imperfect tense-form does not *mean* any of the following categories. Rather, the form can merely be *used* as such in combination with lexical, grammatical, and contextual factors.

- *Progressive* (a past action that unfolded progressively over time): "He <u>was teaching</u> [ἐδίδασκεν] in their synagogues" (Luke 4:15 CSB).
- *Inceptive* (highlights the beginning of an action or state): "[He] picked up his mat, and <u>started to walk</u> [περιεπάτει]" (John 5:9 CSB).
- *Iterative* (a past action that is repeated or customary): "And with many other words he . . . <u>kept on exhorting</u> [παρεκάλει] them" (Acts 2:40 NASB).

1. As was true of the present tense-form, *internal* here means that the action is viewed from within the event rather than in terms of its beginning or end. See Wallace 541.

## CHAPTER 14

- *Tendential* (a past action was begun, attempted, or proposed, but not completed): "and [Paul] tried to persuade [ἔπειθεν] Jews and Greeks" (Acts 18:4).

## Interpretation

Even though Greek has a term meaning "try" or "attempt" (e.g., πειράομαι and πειράζω),[2] the more common method of communicating that concept was to use the imperfect of a verb of effort (destroy, stop, discern, persuade, reconcile, etc.). The imperfect tense-form was used because the imperfective aspect fits well with the idea of repeated attempts being made (as in Gal. 1:13). That is, the action is not described as being complete or as a whole but is portrayed as progressively unfolding over a period of time. This usage is also confirmed by several passages in the NT that clearly convey the idea of an action that was tried or attempted but not successfully completed.

For example, when Jesus came to John to be baptized, we read, "But John tried to stop [διεκώλυεν] Him, saying, 'I need to be baptized by you, and yet you come to me?'" (Matt. 3:14 CSB). We know that John was not successful in stopping Jesus from being baptized by him since the next verse states that John agreed to baptize Jesus (Matt. 3:15). A second example is found in Luke 4:42: "When it was day, he went out and made his way to a deserted place. But the crowds were searching for him. They came to him and tried to keep [κατεῖχον] him from leaving them" (CSB). A few verses later, however, we are told that Jesus continued his preaching ministry in various synagogues in Galilee—signifying that the attempt of the crowd was not successful. Finally, when Jesus was being crucified, the soldiers "tried to give [ἐδίδουν] him wine mixed with myrrh, but he did not take it" (Mark 15:23 CSB). Clearly, the second half of the verse makes it obvious that the effort to give Jesus wine mixed with myrrh failed, since Jesus rejected it.

2. See, e.g., Acts 9:26: "And when he had come to Jerusalem, he attempted [ἐπείρα-ζεν] to join the disciples"; 24:6: "He even tried [ἐπείρασεν] to profane the temple, but we seized him"; 26:21: "For this reason the Jews seized me in the temple and tried [ἐπειρῶντο] to kill me."

Not only is there grammatical and contextual evidence indicating that Paul *attempted* or *tried* to destroy the church but failed (Gal. 1:13); there is also a theological reason. That is, God's purpose and plan cannot fail, and Jesus promised that he will build his church "and the gates of hell shall not prevail against it" (Matt. 16:18). Therefore, even though Paul repeatedly persecuted the church (ἐδίωκον, iterative imperfect, Gal. 1:13), he is not claiming to have destroyed it. Indeed, he later realized that his extreme and violent acts could never overpower God's church. In the end, his repeated attempts were used to propel the message of the gospel. Ultimately Paul himself was overcome by Christ's power, and the very one who sought to destroy Christ's church ended up building it.

# 15

# FUTURE INDICATIVES

## Matthew 4:4

**Introduction**

Temptations are part of life. We all live with them, and we all struggle against giving in to them. When Jesus taught his disciples how to pray, he petitioned, "And lead us not into temptation, but deliver us from evil" (Matt. 6:13). Jesus taught us to pray to the Father that we would be kept from temptations. And yet, we read that it was the Spirit who "drove" (ἐκβάλλει, Mark 1:12) or "led" (ἀνήχθη [from ἀνάγω], Matt. 4:1) Jesus into the wilderness "to be tempted by the devil" (Matt. 4:1). When responding to the traps set by the devil, Jesus quotes the OT, particularly Deuteronomy. In response to the first temptation to turn stones into bread, Jesus says, "Man shall not live [οὐκ ζήσεται] by bread alone, but by every word that comes from the mouth of God" (Matt. 4:4). But what is the function of the future tense? Does it function as an imperative ("man must not live by bread alone") or as a general truth ("one does not live by bread alone," NRSV)?

## Overview

The future tense-form indicates an "occurrence *subsequent* to some reference-point."[1] Or, to put it differently, the future grammaticalizes the author's expectation regarding a possible event, an event that has not yet occurred and thus is future from the author's perspective. The future tense-form rarely occurs outside the indicative mood.[2] Several key uses of the future include the following:

- *Predictive* (predicts a future event): "after three days <u>he will rise</u> [ἀναστήσεται]" (Mark 9:31).
- *Imperatival* (expresses a command): "<u>You shall love</u> [ἀγαπήσεις] your neighbor as yourself" (Matt. 19:19).
- *Deliberative* (asks a real or rhetorical question): "Lord, to whom <u>shall we go</u> [ἀπελευσόμεθα]?" (John 6:68).
- *Gnomic* (conveys a timeless truth): "For each one <u>will bear</u> [βαστάσει] his own load" (Gal. 6:5 NASB).

The future tense-form is often used similarly to an imperative, expressing a command. Most of the NT occurrences of this use are citations of the OT, demonstrating that this usage is strongly influenced by the OT.[3] The imperatival future is most commonly (1) found in the Gospels, especially Matthew, (2) in the second person, and (3) a prohibition (negated with οὐ). In contrast to the imperative mood, the imperatival future often adds an emphatic or solemn notion to the command. The gnomic future "may be used to state what will customarily happen when occasion offers" (Burton, *Syntax*, 36).

1. Buist M. Fanning, *Verbal Aspect in New Testament Greek* (Oxford: Clarendon, 1990), 123.

2. There are twelve future participles: Matt. 27:49; Luke 22:49; John 6:64; Acts 8:27; 20:22; 22:5; 24:11, 17; 1 Cor. 15:37; Heb. 3:5; Heb. 13:17; 1 Pet. 3:13. A possible thirteenth future participle is in Rom. 8:34. There are five future infinitives: Acts 11:28; 23:30; 24:15; 27:10; Heb. 3:18.

3. The imperatival future, however, is found in Classical Greek: BDF §362, p. 183; Ernest DeWitt Burton, *Syntax of the Moods and Tenses in New Testament Greek*, 3rd ed. (Edinburgh: T&T Clark, 1898), 35; D&M 19; Porter, *Idioms*, 44; Wallace 569.

## Interpretation

The three temptations of Jesus (according to Matthew's Gospel) are as follows:

| | | | |
|---|---|---|---|
| **First Test** | The devil | "If you are the Son of God, command these stones to become loaves of bread" (Matt. 4:3). | |
| | Jesus | "It is written, 'Man <u>shall</u> not <u>live</u> [ζήσεται] by bread alone, but by every word that comes from the mouth of God'" (Matt. 4:4). | Deut. 8:3 |
| **Second Test** | The devil | "If you are the Son of God, throw yourself down, for it is written, '<u>He will command</u> [ἐντελεῖται] his angels concerning you,' and 'On their hands <u>they will bear</u> you <u>up</u> [ἀροῦσιν], lest you strike your foot against a stone'" (Matt. 4:6). | Ps. 91:11–12 |
| | Jesus | "Again it is written, '<u>You shall</u> not <u>put</u> the Lord your God <u>to the test</u> [ἐκπειράσεις]'" (Matt. 4:7). | Deut. 6:16 |
| **Third Test** | The devil | "All these <u>I will give</u> [δώσω] you, if you will fall down and worship me" (Matt. 4:9). | |
| | Jesus | "Be gone, Satan! For it is written, '<u>You shall worship</u> [προσκυνήσεις] the Lord your God and him only <u>shall you serve</u> [λατρεύσεις]'" (Matt. 4:10). | Deut. 6:13 |

The question before us is whether the future verb ζήσεται in Matthew 4:4 is imperatival or gnomic. Is the verb functioning as a command ("Don't live by bread alone") or is it merely stating a general principle ("People don't live by bread alone")? There are several reasons to favor the former over the latter.[4] First, the imperatival future is used in Jesus's other two citations. In the second test, Jesus responds, "<u>You shall</u> not <u>put</u> the Lord your God <u>to the test</u> [ἐκπειράσεις]" (4:7), and in the third test he replies, "<u>You shall worship</u> [προσκυνήσεις] the Lord your God and him only <u>shall you serve</u> [λατρεύσεις]" (4:10). All three of these futures are clearly imperatival.[5]

4. Burton (*Syntax*, 35) maintains that the imperatival function is "probable," and Robertson (889) claims it is "possible." Cf. M&E (138) and Young (119), who take it as gnomic.

5. Note that the two futures in Matt. 4:6 are predictive futures: The devil, quoting Ps. 91:11–12, declares, "'<u>He will command</u> [ἐντελεῖται] his angels concerning you,' and 'On their hands <u>they will bear</u> you <u>up</u> [ἀροῦσιν], lest you strike your foot against a stone'" (Matt. 4:6). Jesus's response reminds us that God's promises never conflict

Second, most English versions opt for the imperatival nuance over the gnomic, although the following versions render the future as gnomic:

- NRSV: "One does not live by bread alone."
- NET: "Man does not live by bread alone."
- NJB: "Human beings live not on bread alone."
- NLT: "People do not live by bread alone."

These versions should be seriously considered, but most of the more popular or well-known versions opt for the imperatival sense:

- ESV, KJV, NKJV, RSV: "Man *shall not live* by bread alone."
- CSB: "Man *must not live* on bread alone."
- NASB, NIV: Man *shall not live* on bread alone."

Third, the statement does not really sound like an omnitemporal or timeless truth. Although the first part of the saying might have a proverbial sense, the second part does not. It is simply not true that people normally live by the words that proceed from God, although this *should* be the case.

Finally, the imperatival usage is far more common than the gnomic use.[6] In fact, Wallace (571) notes that the gnomic is "very rarely used"

---

with his commands. The devil also uses a predictive future in 4:9: "All these I will give [δώσω] you, if you will fall down and worship me."

6. The following is a nearly comprehensive list of the imperatival futures in the NT:

a. Imperatival future quoting the Ten Commandments: φονεύσεις (Matt. 5:21; 19:18; Rom. 13:9); μοιχεύσεις (Matt. 5:27; 19:18; Rom. 13:9); κλέψεις (Matt. 19:18; Rom. 13:9); ψευδομαρτυρήσεις (Matt. 19:18); ἐπιθυμήσεις (Rom. 7:7; 13:9).

b. Imperatival future quoting Leviticus: ἔσεσθε (1 Pet. 1:16; quoting Lev. 11:44–45); ἐπιορκήσεις (Matt. 5:33; quoting Lev. 19:12); ἀγαπήσεις (Matt. 22:39; Rom. 13:9; Gal. 5:14; James 2:8; quoting Lev. 19:18); ἀγαπήσεις, μισήσεις (Matt. 5:43; quoting Lev. 19:18).

c. Imperatival future quoting Deuteronomy: ἀγαπήσεις (Matt. 22:37; Mark 12:30; Luke 10:27; quoting Deut. 6:5); προσκυνήσεις (Matt. 4:10; Luke 4:8; quoting Deut. 6:13); ἐκπειράσεις (Matt. 4:7; Luke 4:12; quoting Deut. 6:16); ζήσεται (Matt. 4:4; quoting Deut. 8:3); φιμώσεις (1 Tim. 5:18; quoting Deut. 25:4).

d. Imperatival future quoting Isaiah: κληθήσεται (Matt. 21:13; quoting Isa. 56:7).

in the NT, and B&W (98) indicate that there appear to be only four uses in the NT (Rom. 5:7; 7:3; Gal. 6:5; Eph. 5:31).

One argument against the use of the imperatival function is that the verb in Matthew 4:4 (ζήσεται) is a third-person verb, whereas most of the occurrences of the imperatival future are second person. There are, however, several clear uses of the third person (Matt. 20:26–27; 21:13; 23:11; Mark 9:35; 10:44)[7] and others that may fall into this category (e.g., Matt. 16:22; Rom. 6:14; Gal. 6:5).[8]

e. Imperatival future not quoting the OT: καλέσεις (Matt. 1:21; Luke 1:13, 31); ἔσεσθε (Matt. 5:48; 6:5); ἔσται (Matt. 20:26–27 [3×]; Mark 9:35; see also Matt. 23:11; Mark 10:44); ἐρεῖτε (Matt. 21:3); ὄψῃ (Matt. 27:4); ὄψεσθε (Matt. 27:24; Acts 18:15); ἀφήσεις (Luke 17:4); ἀρκεσθησόμεθα (1 Tim. 6:8).
7. See also the first-person use in 1 Tim. 6:8.
8. For those who favor interpreting Rom. 6:14 as an imperatival future, see Tyndale's translation and B&W 97; for the possibility of Gal. 6:5, see KMP 273n64; B&W 98.

# 16

# AORIST INDICATIVES

## Ephesians 4:20

### Introduction

In 1972 Frank Stagg published an article titled "The Abused Aorist."[1] In this essay he sought to dispel a common misunderstanding about the aorist tense-form; namely, that the aorist conveys a once-for-all, or punctiliar, type of action.[2] He provided examples from commentaries and grammars that fell prey to this stereotyped misconception. It is, however, possible for the aorist to convey a singular event,[3] but such a conclusion is not based on the verb tense itself but upon the lexical meaning of the verb and the context. In Ephesians 4, Paul contrasts the mind-set and lifestyle of unbelieving Gentiles with those to whom he writes, reminding them that they have learned a far different way. He writes, "But that is not the way <u>you learned</u> [ἐμάθετε] Christ!" (Eph. 4:20). In using the aorist form, is Paul indicating that this verb should be viewed as a onetime action or a single event such

1. Frank Stagg, "The Abused Aorist," *JBL* 91 (1972): 222–31.
2. Over forty years later, Stagg's essay was followed by David L. Mathewson, "The Abused Present," *BBR* 23, no. 3 (2013): 343–63.
3. See, e.g., Rom. 6:10: "<u>He died</u> [ἀπέθανεν] to sin, once for all."

as conversion? Or can the verb communicate a summary statement that would allow an undetermined period of time?

## Overview

The aorist indicative is the most common tense-form in the NT. Fundamentally, the aorist is used when the author desires to portray the action in its entirety without reference to its progress or duration. The aorist is also the default tense-form used in narratives, often carrying the main story line of the narrative. In about 80 percent of the uses, the time of the action for the aorist is in the past, which is communicated by the addition of the augment at the beginning of the verb. The following categories relate not to the meaning of the aorist tense-form but to the use of the aorist in combination with lexical, grammatical, and contextual factors.

- *Constative* (portrays the action in its entirety without regard to the process or duration): "Then he stayed [ἐνέμεινεν] two whole years" (Acts 28:30 HCSB).
- *Inceptive* (emphasizes the commencement of an action or a state): "Jesus began to weep [ἐδάκρυσεν]" (John 11:35 NRSV).
- *Culminative* (emphasizes the cessation of an action or state): "He brought [ἤγαγεν] him to Jesus" (John 1:42).
- *Epistolary* (depicts a present action [usually "writing" or "sending"] from the perspective of the readers by using the aorist instead of the present): "But now I am writing [ἔγραψα] to you" (1 Cor. 5:11).
- *Gnomic* (conveys a universal statement or one that is generally true): "The grass withers [ἐξηράνθη]" (1 Pet. 1:24).

## Interpretation

Precisely how is the aorist verb ἐμάθετε used in Ephesians 4:20, "But that is not the way you learned Christ!"? Some commentators press the aorist so that it must refer to a distinct point-in-time action. This is the position of Ernest Best, who comments, "The aorist tense of the verb probably indicates the moment or period when they became Christians."[4] In verse 21 Paul adds, "assuming that <u>you have heard</u> (ἠκούσατε) about him and <u>were taught</u> (ἐδιδάχθητε) in him, as the truth is in Jesus." These two additional verbs ("heard" and "were taught") expand what took place when the Ephesians "learned" the truths of the Christian faith. Explaining the significance of the aorist ἠκούσατε (heard), Best continues, "The aorist tense suggests the hearing is that of the time of conversion" (427). Similarly, regarding the aorist ἐδιδάχθητε (were taught), he notes, "The aorist suggests it refers to a past period of teaching, often understood as a time of initial catechetical instruction. . . . The aorist tense, with its suggestion of a fixed period, is inappropriate to such ongoing [postbaptismal] teaching" (427–28). Then he asks why the aorist is used and answers: "The two verbs of hearing and being taught may refer to the same event of becoming a Christian looked at from distinct angles. Acceptance of Christ implies not only some relation to him but also acceptance of some understanding of who he is and what he has done, i.e., the acceptance of some body, however slender, of doctrine" (428).

Harold Hoehner follows a similar interpretation regarding the verb ἐμάθετε. Hoehner, however, does not state that the aorist conveys a onetime action but rather maintains that the aorist form in this context conveys the entrance into an action. He states, "The inceptive aorist points to the time of conversion. Gentiles and Jews who had previously opposed God, heard Christ preached and received him. This then is the beginning point of their 'learning Christ.'"[5] Likewise, he affirms that the aorist ἠκούσατε (heard) "points to the time of conversion as it does in verse 20" (*Ephesians*, 595). He differs from Best regarding the third aorist ἐδιδάχθητε (were taught), which he claims "occurs not only at conversion but through daily growth by increased knowledge of [Christ]" (595). Thus he affirms that this verb is "most likely a constative aorist" (595).

It is best, however, to view both ἐμάθετε and ἐδιδάχθητε as constative aorists. This category "describes the action in summary fashion,

4. Ernest Best, *Ephesians*, ICC (London: T&T Clark, 1998), 427.
5. Harold W. Hoehner, *Ephesians: An Exegetical Commentary* (Grand Rapids: Baker Academic, 2002), 594.

without focusing on the beginning or end of the action specifically" (Wallace 557). The idea, then, is not that the aorist tense-form is pinpointing a particular time in history but that it is portraying the action in its entirety without regard to the process or time it took to accomplish the action. Lincoln argues that ἐδιδάχθητε "highlights the *further stage* of catechesis," rejecting the idea that the aorist tense-form points to the time of conversion.[6] Likewise Thielman comments, "Paul assumes that after his readers heard and believed the gospel, they *continued* to learn more about the Christian tradition."[7] Thus Larkin is certainly correct in writing, "A point in time event like conversion reads too much into the aorist tense."[8]

Interestingly, Hoehner takes the first verb ("learned") as an inceptive aorist, whereas he takes the second verb ("were taught") as constative. The reason this distinction should be rejected is that both verbs refer to the same event, just from different perspectives. Indeed, Lincoln rightly states that being taught is "the other side of learning about him and involves receiving instruction in the gospel tradition."[9]

Being a disciple of Jesus is not something that is completed at the time of conversion. It is not simply about learning mere facts about Christ. Rather, it involves a lifetime of learning and growing, as believers continually seek to conform to the image of Christ. It includes knowing Christ himself and being taught by him through the Spirit and the word. It is about knowing him firsthand, which includes living a life that is distinct from those who have never encountered the living Messiah.

6. Andrew T. Lincoln, *Ephesians*, WBC 42 (Dallas: Word, 1990), 280, emphasis added.

7. Frank Thielman, *Ephesians*, BECNT (Grand Rapids: Baker Academic, 2010), 301, emphasis added.

8. William J. Larkin, *Ephesians: A Handbook on the Greek Text*, Baylor Handbook on the Greek New Testament (Waco: Baylor University Press, 2009), 90.

9. Lincoln, *Ephesians*, 280. It is possible that the verb ἠκούσατε refers "primarily to the readers' initial reception of this message . . . [and] draws attention primarily to the first stage of its transmission" (280). Such a distinction, however, is based on the lexical meaning of the verbs and the context and not the aorist tense-form.

# 17

# PERFECT AND PLUPERFECT INDICATIVES

## John 19:30

## Introduction

John 19:30 states, "When Jesus had received the sour wine, he said, 'It is finished,' and he bowed his head and gave up his spirit." The declaration "It is finished" is the English translation of a single Greek word, τετέλεσται, the perfect passive of τελέω. Mounce maintains, "This one-word summary of Jesus's life and death is perhaps the single most important statement in all of Scripture."[1] But what is the full significance of this statement? Is Jesus looking back over his life and making a claim about how he has fulfilled all that was prophesied about him? Or is Jesus looking ahead to the present blessings that would come as a result of his death and resurrection?

1. William D. Mounce, *Basics of Biblical Greek*, 4th ed. (Grand Rapids: Zondervan, 2019), 275.

## Overview

The perfect tense-form can be described as conveying a completed action that has continuing results. In other words, the action was performed in the past and has been completed, yet the resulting consequences of that action still continue into the present (from the author's time frame). Thus γέγραπται does not simply mean "It has been written" (which focuses on the past action) but "It is written" (which implies that something was written in the past yet still has abiding implications for today). The aspect of the perfect is typically described as stative, which focuses on the state of being that results from a previous action. Some have described the perfect as a combination of the aorist (perfective aspect) and the present (imperfective aspect).[2] It is often helpful for the interpreter to determine which of these two features is being emphasized in a particular context. That is, sometimes the focus is on the past completed action (translated with the helping verb "have/has") and other times the emphasis is on the resulting state caused by the action (translated more like a present tense verb).

- *Consummative* (emphasizes the completed action that produced the resulting state): "If we say <u>we have not sinned</u> [ἡμαρτήκαμεν]" (1 John 1:10).

- *Intensive* (emphasizes the resulting state brought about by a past action): "<u>It is written</u> [γέγραπται] in the book of the prophets" (Acts 7:42).

- *Dramatic* (vividly depicts a past event or state): "John testified about Him and <u>cried out</u> [κέκραγεν]" (John 1:15 NASB).

- *Present state* (conveys a present meaning when used with certain verbs that lost their perfect significance): "Now <u>we know</u> [ἐγνώκαμεν] that you have a demon!" (John 8:52).

- *Gnomic* (communicates a general or customary truth): "A wife <u>is bound</u> [δέδεται] as long as her husband is living" (1 Cor. 7:39 CSB).

---

2. See KMP 231; Nicholas J. Ellis, "Aspect-Prominence, Morpho-Syntax, and a Cognitive-Linguistic Framework for the Greek Verb," in *The Greek Verb Revisited: A Fresh Approach for Biblical Exegesis*, ed. Steven E. Runge and Christopher J. Fresch (Bellingham, WA: Lexham, 2016), 122–60.

The pluperfect can be described as a past state that was caused by a previous action.[3] That is, when a narrator describes an event in the past (typically using the aorist) and then wants to mention an event that occurred prior to that event, the pluperfect is often used. For example, in the Sermon on the Mount, Jesus proclaims that a wise person is one who hears and does his words. Such a person is likened to a person who builds their house on a solid foundation. He states, "The rain fell [aor.], and the floods came [aor.], and the winds blew [aor.] and beat [aor.] on that house, but it did not fall [aor.], because it had been founded [τεθεμελίωτο, plupf.] on the rock" (Matt. 7:25). Prior to the rain, floods, and wind coming, the house had been built on a solid foundation. The aspectual significance of the pluperfect emphasizes the resulting (past) state of a previous action or event. The pluperfect is not common, occurring only eighty-six times in the NT, and is found only in the indicative.

- *Consummative* (emphasizes the completion of a past action): "Now the betrayer had given [δεδώκει] them a sign" (Mark 14:44).
- *Intensive* (emphasizes the past results brought about by a past action): "It was [ἐγεγόνει] now dark, and Jesus had not yet come to them" (John 6:17).
- *Past state* (with certain verbs conveys a past state with no antecedent action): "The whole crowd stood [εἱστήκει] on the beach" (Matt. 13:2).

### Interpretation

The question before us is whether τετέλεσται of John 19:30 is a consummative perfect (emphasizing the past action that brought about the current state) or an intensive perfect (emphasizing the present state that results from the past action). In other words, was Jesus "looking backward to the state of affairs that had just been drawn to a close: the OT sacrifices, rituals, typology, as well as His own

---

3. The pluperfect conveys "a *past* state of affairs constituted by an action still further in the past." Zerwick, *Bib. Gk.*, §290, p. 98.

life and sufferings" (Young 127–28)? Or was Jesus "looking ahead to the benefits of His death, . . . [i.e.,] the continuing state of a debt that has forever been paid and which is available to all" (Young 128)? Although to some extent both are true, the emphasis lies on the first option (the consummative perfect).

1. John's Gospel highlights the importance of Jesus accomplishing the work that the Father has given him. For example, in John 17:4 Jesus states, "I glorified you on earth, having accomplished the work that you gave me to do."[4]

2. The same Greek word (τετέλεσται) is used only two verses earlier (19:28) and clearly refers to fulfilling OT Scripture: "After this, Jesus, knowing that all <u>was</u> now <u>finished</u> [τετέλεσται], said (<u>to fulfill</u> [τελειωθῇ] the Scripture), 'I thirst.'" Most likely the Scripture to which Jesus alludes is Psalm 69:21. So in verse 30 when Jesus states "It is finished," John is demonstrating by the repetition of the word that the two verses should be interpreted together. In addition, John does not use the typical word translated "fulfill" (i.e., πληρωθῇ, from πληρόω), but instead uses the verb τελειόω which comes from the same Greek word group (τελ-). Thus John is stressing how Jesus is the fulfillment of the OT.

3. The lexical meaning of τελέω (bring to an end, finish, complete) and the perfect tense-form combine to emphasize the completion of Jesus's mission. Young (128) rightly argues, "The verbal idea in τετέλεσται argues heavily in favor of a consummative perfect."[5] At the same time, we must remember that both aspects of the perfect (the completed action and the enduring state) are affirmed by the perfect tense-form.[6]

---

4. See also John 4:34, "My food is to do the will of him who sent me and to accomplish his work"; and 5:36, "For the works that the Father has given me to accomplish, the very works that I am doing, bear witness about me that the Father has sent me."

5. Contra Murray J. Harris, who states specifically regarding the verb in 19:28, "The emphasis is on the state resulting from a past occurrence." *John*, EGGNT (Nashville: B&H, 2015), 316.

6. Edward W. Klink III writes, "The nature of the completed action is magnified by the verb's perfect tense, which describes a past action with continuingly present-tense force." *John*, ZECNT (Grand Rapids: Zondervan, 2016), 811.

On at least two occasions Charles Spurgeon preached a sermon based on John 19:30. In the first sermon, titled "It Is Finished" and preached on December 1, 1861, Spurgeon highlighted five ways in which Christ finished his work: (1) all the types, promises, and prophecies were now fully accomplished in him; (2) all the typical sacrifices of the old Jewish law were now abolished, as well as explained; (3) Christ's perfect obedience was finished; (4) the satisfaction that Christ rendered to the justice of God was finished; and (5) Jesus had totally destroyed the power of Satan, of sin, and of death. Spurgeon expounds the first point as follows:

> All the Scripture was now fulfilled, that when He said, "It is finished!" the whole book, from first to the last, in both the law and the prophets, was finished in Him! There is not a single jewel of promise, from that first emerald which fell on the threshold of Eden, to that last sapphire of Malachi, which was not set in the breastplate of the true High Priest. No, there is not a type, from the red heifer downward to the turtle dove, from the hyssop upwards to Solomon's temple itself, which was not fulfilled in Him; and not a prophecy, whether spoken on Chebar's bank, or in the shore of the Jordan, which was not now fully worked out in Christ Jesus![7]

In other words, "This one Greek word is the final statement of God, declaring that everything he wanted to accomplish has been completed to perfection in the person and work of his Son" (Klink, *John*, 811).

---

7. Charles H. Spurgeon, "It Is Finished," *Metropolitan Tabernacle Pulpit*, no. 421.

# 18

# SUBJUNCTIVE MOOD

## Hebrews 13:5

### Introduction

In 2 Timothy 3:16 we are told that "all Scripture is breathed out by God" and is therefore "profitable." And yet we sometimes wonder if some verses or passages in the Bible are more important, relevant, or powerful than others. For example, could it be said that Hebrews 13:5 ("I will never leave you nor forsake you") is one of the most powerful verses in the Bible? If so, on what basis would someone make this claim?

### Overview

Some have described the subjunctive mood as the mood of uncertainty.[1] While it is sometimes true that a subjunctive represents something that is uncertain, such is not always the case. For example, John employs the subjunctive to describe the return of Christ: "so that

---

1. For example, Curtis Vaughan and Virtus E. Gideon explain that the subjunctive mood "is used for doubtful, hesitating assertions." *A Greek Grammar of the New Testament* (Nashville: Broadman, 1979), 102. See also William Hersey Davis, *Beginner's Grammar of the Greek New Testament* (New York: Harper & Row, 1923), 74.

when he appears [ἐὰν φανερωθῇ] we may have confidence and not shrink from him in shame at his coming" (1 John 2:28) and "when he appears [ἐὰν φανερωθῇ] we shall be like him, because we shall see him as he is" (1 John 3:2). John uses the subjunctive mood not because the return of Christ is uncertain, but because the time of his return is unknown to us and therefore is indefinite.

It is best, therefore, not to describe the subjunctive mood as the mood of uncertainty but as "indefinite but probable" (the mood of probability). Despite the tense-form used, the action of the subjunctive mood typically occurs in the future. In contrast to the future indicative, however, the subjunctive often deals with something that *might* take place in the future, whereas the future indicative usually indicates something that *will* take place (at least as portrayed by the one who is making the statement). There are various uses of the subjunctive mood:

- *Purpose/result* (ἵνα or ὅπως + subjunctive): "Now all this took place to fulfill [ἵνα πληρωθῇ] what was spoken by the Lord through the prophet" (Matt. 1:22 CSB).
- *Conditional* (ἐάν or ἐὰν μή + subjunctive): "If anyone thirsts [ἐάν . . . διψᾷ], let him come to me and drink" (John 7:37).
- *Indefinite relative* (ὅσ[τις] ἄν/ἐάν or ὃς [δ'] ἄν + subjunctive): "but whoever keeps [ὃς δ' ἄν τηρῇ] his word, in him truly the love of God is perfected" (1 John 2:5).
- *Temporal relative* (ὅταν [or ἕως, ἄχρι, μέχρι] + subjunctive): "Consider it a great joy, my brothers, whenever you experience [ὅταν . . . περιπέσητε] various trials" (James 1:2 HCSB).
- *Hortatory* (first-person plural subjunctive functioning as an imperative): "Therefore, let us approach [προσερχώμεθα] the throne of grace with boldness" (Heb. 4:16 CSB).
- *Deliberative* (asks a real or rhetorical question): "What shall I say [εἴπω] to you?" (1 Cor. 11:22).
- *Emphatic negation* (double negative, οὐ μή): "I give them eternal life, and they will never perish [οὐ μὴ ἀπόλωνται]" (John 10:28).

## CHAPTER 18

- *Prohibitory* (a negated aorist subjunctive that functions as an imperative): "And <u>do not bring</u> [μὴ εἰσενέγκῃς] us into temptation" (Matt. 6:13 CSB).

## Interpretation

As mentioned above, the subjunctive mood does not necessarily communicate uncertainty. As a matter of fact, sometimes the subjunctive mood communicates something that is emphatically certain (that is, something that certainly will *not* happen). Such is the case with "emphatic negation," which is expressed by the double negative οὐ μή (the indicative and nonindicative negative particles) plus the aorist subjunctive (or occasionally the future indicative). As the name suggests, this type of negation is emphatic and strongly denies that something will occur. In fact, it "is the strongest way to negate something in Greek" (Wallace 468). Interestingly, about 90 percent of the NT uses are found in the sayings of Jesus or in citations from the Septuagint.

One example of emphatic negation is found in Hebrews 13:5b: οὐ μή σε ἀνῶ οὐδ' οὐ μή σε ἐγκαταλίπω, "I will never leave you nor [never] forsake you." In context, the author claims that the basis of our contentment and freedom from the love of money is that God promises always to be with us and never to forsake us. This verse is a possible conflation of Genesis 28:15; Deuteronomy 31:6–8; and/or Joshua 1:5. The message is that the covenant-keeping God promises to continually provide for his people.

But, grammatically speaking, can this verse be considered one of the most powerful verses in the Bible? The reason some may answer yes to this question is that it contains five negatives (two emphatic negations plus the conjunction οὐδέ, "nor"). This idea is captured well in the old hymn "How Firm a Foundation." The last verse reads,

> The soul that on Jesus has leaned for repose,
> I will not, I will not desert to its foes;
> That soul, though all hell should endeavor to shake,
> I'll *never, no never, no never* forsake.[2]

2. The author of this hymn is unknown. It is found in John Rippon's hymnal (*A Selection of Hymns from the Best Authors*), but where the author's name is normally

Charles Spurgeon often referred to this text in his sermons and preached this text on more than one occasion, as in a sermon titled "Never! Never! Never! Never! Never!"

> I have no doubt you are aware that our translation does not convey the whole force of the original, and that it would hardly be possible in English to give the full weight of the Greek. We might render it, "He hath said, I will never, never leave thee; I will never, never, never forsake thee"; for, though that would be not a literal, but rather a free rendering, yet, as there are five negatives in the Greek, we do not know how to give their force in any other way. Two negatives nullify each other in our language; but here, in the Greek, they intensify the meaning following one after another.[3]

About ten years later Spurgeon again returned to this text.

> In our English language, two negatives would destroy each other, but it is not so in the Greek language—and the heaping up, as it were, of these denials on God's part of all thought of ever forsaking His people ought to be sufficient to satisfy even the most doubtful among us! If God has said, "I will not, not, NOT, no never forsake My people," we must believe Him! And we must chase away all thought of the possibility of the Lord's forsaking His servants, or leaving them to perish.[4]

Although not formally trained, Spurgeon taught himself Greek and knew that studying the Greek text would improve his preaching. We would do well to follow his example by paying attention to the original text so that we hear (and feel!) the full weight of God's message to us.

---

listed, only the initial *K* appears. Some think that this is a reference to the music director Robert Keene at Carter's Lane Baptist Church in London, where Rippon was a pastor for more than fifty years.

3. "Never! Never! Never! Never! Never!," no. 477, delivered on Sunday morning, October 26, 1862, by Rev. C. H. Spurgeon at the Metropolitan Tabernacle, Newington, England.

4. "Never, No Never, No Never," no. 3150, delivered on Sunday evening, March 16, 1873, at the Metropolitan Tabernacle, Newington, England.

# 19

# IMPERATIVE MOOD

## Matthew 6:11

### Introduction

When Jesus taught his disciples how to pray, he prayed:

> Our Father in heaven,
>   hallowed be [ἁγιασθήτω] your name.
> Your kingdom come [ἐλθέτω],
>   your will be done [γενηθήτω],
>     on earth as it is in heaven.
> Give [δός] us this day our daily bread,
> and forgive [ἄφες] us our debts,
>   as we also have forgiven our debtors.
> And lead us not [μὴ εἰσενέγκῃς] into temptation,
> but deliver [ῥῦσαι] us from evil. (Matt. 6:9–13)

In this prayer, seven imperatives are used,[1] all of them in the aorist tense-form. The first three petitions are focused on God, and the final four focus on those praying. This shift is evidenced by the change from third-person imperatives to second-person imperatives as well

---

1. Technically, there are six imperatives and one prohibitory subjunctive, μὴ εἰσενέγκῃς.

84

as a switch from the second-person personal pronoun "your" (σου) to the first-person "our" (ἡμῶν). Because it is a prayer, these imperatives are classified as requests (see below), but the question before us is the function of the aorist. Why are aorist imperatives used, especially when many of these requests are for things we need on an ongoing basis? Regarding the imperative in 6:11 ("Give [δός] us this day our daily bread"), Wallace (720) suggests, "This is also both urgent and momentary." But is that the best way to understand why the aorist tense-form is used? Was the aorist used in this context because the request was urgent or momentary?

## Overview

The imperative mood typically expresses a command. It can also be described as the mood of intention since it is used in contexts other than a command. According to D&M (174), "It expresses neither probability nor possibility, but only intention, and is, therefore, the furthest removed from reality." The following categories represent the main uses of the imperative mood:

- *Command* (an exhortation or charge): "In everything <u>give thanks</u> [εὐχαριστεῖτε]" (1 Thess. 5:18 NASB).
- *Prohibition* (a negative command that forbids an action): "<u>Do not be deceived</u> [μὴ πλανᾶσθε]" (1 Cor. 15:33).
- *Request* (a plea given to a superior): "Lord, [please] <u>help</u> [βοήθει] me" (Matt. 15:25).
- *Permission* (expresses permission, allowance, or toleration): "<u>Let him do</u> [ποιείτω] as he wishes" (1 Cor. 7:36).
- *Conditional* (an implied conditional statement): "<u>Destroy</u> [λύσατε] this temple, and in three days I will raise it up" (John 2:19).

## Interpretation

When an author desired to communicate a command that was to be done on a specific occasion (single occurrence), the aorist tense-form was typically used.[2] Conversely, when an author desired to communicate a command that was to be done as a general precept (multiple occurrences), the present tense-form was typically used. Although there are exceptions, this noticeable pattern is a helpful guideline. Indeed, the specific command (with aorist imperatives) versus general precept (with present imperatives) is affirmed by most grammarians.[3] This guideline helps explain why aorist imperatives are more frequent in narratives, whereas present imperatives are more frequent in epistles. Because narratives typically report the events that took place between particular individuals or groups, a specific command is expected.

There is also a natural relationship between a verb's aspect and the specific command / general precept distinction. Because the perfective aspect (aorist tense-form) communicates an author's portrayal of an action in its entirety or as a whole, it is natural for this aspect to be used when communicating a specific command since such an action is to be done in its entirety on that particular occasion. Conversely, because the imperfective aspect (present tense-form) communicates an author's portrayal of an action in progress or ongoing, it is natural for this aspect to be used when communicating a general precept, since such an action is to be repeated on appropriate occasions (customary).

So, why is the aorist tense-form used in the Lord's Prayer when the petitions are not just single occurrences? The main answer to this question is *literary genre*. That is, the aorist imperative is greatly favored in prayers, even when it is used to refer to something general in nature. In other texts, present imperatives are normally used to command or forbid a general behavior (general precept), whereas the aorist is used to command or forbid an action on a specific occasion

2. Some of the material in this chapter appears in Benjamin L. Merkle, "Verbal Aspect and Imperatives: Ephesians as a Test Case," in *New Testament Philology: Essays in Honor of David Alan Black*, ed. Melton Bennett Winstead (Eugene, OR: Wipf & Stock, 2018), 34–51.

3. See, e.g., BDF §335, p. 172; Buist M. Fanning, *Verbal Aspect in New Testament Greek* (Oxford: Clarendon, 1990), 327–40; Fanning, "Approaches to Verbal Aspect in New Testament Greek: Issues in Definition and Method," in *Biblical Greek Language and Linguistics: Open Questions in Current Research*, ed. Stanley E. Porter and D. A. Carson (Sheffield: Sheffield Academic, 1993), 55; Wallace 719–22; Zerwick, *Bib. Gk.*, §243, p. 79.

(specific command). In prayers, however, where imperatives are used to make requests to God, the predominant tense-form is the aorist, whether referring to a general precept or a specific occasion. In these cases, the literary genre (prayer) virtually determines the use of the tense-form.[4]

Thus the use of the aorist imperatives should not be overinterpreted. For example, Rogers and Rogers state that the aorist looks "at a specific request."[5] Actually, this is a daily (and thus repeated) prayer that would fit more naturally with the present tense-form. The aorist is used because the verb form is found in a prayer and is a telic verb. Interestingly, Luke uses the present tense-form (δίδου) in his version of the prayer (11:3), most likely because he uses "each day" (ESV) or "day by day" (καθ' ἡμέραν, e.g., NKJV) instead of "today" (σήμερον, CEB). This is one of the rare exceptions where an aorist form is not used in a prayer.

Osborne, following Porter, suggests that the aorist imperative looks "at the action as a single whole."[6] But it is more likely that this usage reflects the literary genre (prayer) and the verb's lexical nature rather than the author's intent to offer a particular perspective regarding the action. It is also probably going too far to claim that the aorist is used to convey an urgent request. In the end, the genre is the determining factor for why the aorist tense-form was selected.

---

4. See, e.g., S. M. Baugh, *Introduction to Greek Tense Form Choice in the Non-indicative Moods*, PDF ed. (Escondido, CA, 2009), 41–42, https://dailydoseofgreek .com/wp-content/uploads/sites/2/2015/09/GreekTenseFormChoice-Baugh.pdf, used with permission; Willem Frederik Bakker, *The Greek Imperative: An Investigation into the Aspectual Differences between the Present and Aorist Imperatives in Greek Prayer from Homer up to the Present Day* (Amsterdam: Hakkert, 1966); Fanning, *Verbal Aspect in New Testament Greek*, 380; Wallace 487–88, 720.

5. Cleon L. Rogers Jr. and Cleon L. Rogers, *The New Linguistic and Exegetical Key to the Greek New Testament* (Grand Rapids: Zondervan, 1998), 13.

6. Grant R. Osborne, *Matthew*, ZECNT (Grand Rapids: Zondervan, 2010), 228n22.

# 20

# OPTATIVE MOOD

## 1 Corinthians 6:15

### Introduction

It is easy to miscommunicate if we are not careful with our words. In one of my first sermons, I preached on Romans 7:7–12. In this text, Paul asks a rhetorical question, "Is the Law sin?" (7:7 NASB). At this point Paul emphatically denies this statement by using the optative mood. He cries, "May it never be!" (μὴ γένοιτο, NASB). In explaining the meaning of this statement, I told the congregation that Paul uses this phrase when nothing could be further from the truth. I then proceeded to give the rendering of this phrase in various translations. I stated, "May it never be!" (NASB), "Certainly not!" (NIV), "By no means!" (RSV), and then I said, "And 'God forbid' if you use the King James Version." What I meant is that the KJV renders μὴ γένοιτο as "God forbid," but apparently that was not what I communicated. After the service, a woman approached me and pointedly asked if I meant to say that a person should not use the KJV. Thankfully, I was able to clarify my point. But what exactly does Paul mean by this phrase, and how is it best translated?

## Overview

The optative mood is often described as the mood of possibility (whereas the subjunctive mood is described as the mood of probability). It can be viewed as a weakened subjunctive (Robertson 936). According to D&M (172), "It contains no definite anticipation of realization, but merely presents the action as conceivable." During the Koine period, the optative was dying out, becoming replaced by the subjunctive. As a result, there are only 68 uses of the optative in the NT (45 aorist forms, and 23 present forms). Most of the uses are found in Luke and Paul, often to express a prayer/benediction, wish, or blessing (i.e., the voluntative optative). When negated, it expresses abhorrence (e.g., μὴ γένοιτο). All but one of the forms are third-person singular (Philem. 20 is the exception, with a first-person singular form: ὀναίμην, "May I benefit from you in the Lord," CSB).

- *Benediction*: "May mercy, peace, and love be multiplied [πληθυνθείη] to you" (Jude 2).
- *Prayer/request*: "May it not be charged [λογισθείη] against them!" (2 Tim. 4:16).
- *Blessing*: "Now may the Lord of peace himself give [δῴη] you peace at all times in every way" (2 Thess. 3:16).
- *Abhorrence*: "Are we to continue in sin that grace may abound? By no means [μὴ γένοιτο]!" (Rom. 6:1–2).

## Interpretation

The phrase μὴ γένοιτο is used 15 times in the NT (14 times in Paul, and once in Luke). As stated above, it is typically found in response to a rhetorical question that is asked but then is categorically and definitively answered in the negative. Below are Paul's questions that are answered with this phrase:

- "What if some were unfaithful? Does their faithlessness nullify the faithfulness of God?" (Rom. 3:3)

- "But if our unrighteousness serves to show the righteousness of God, what shall we say? That God is unrighteous to inflict wrath on us?" (Rom. 3:5)
- "Do we then overthrow the law by this faith?" (Rom. 3:31)
- "Are we to continue in sin that grace may abound?" (Rom. 6:1)
- "Are we to sin because we are not under law but under grace?" (Rom. 6:15)
- "Is the Law sin?" (Rom. 7:7 NASB)
- "Did that which is good, then, bring death to me?" (Rom. 7:13)
- "What shall we say then? Is there injustice on God's part?" (Rom. 9:14)
- "I ask, then, has God rejected his people?" (Rom. 11:1)
- "So I ask, did they stumble in order that they might fall?" (Rom. 11:11)
- "Do you not know that your bodies are members of Christ? Shall I then take the members of Christ and make them members of a prostitute?" (1 Cor. 6:15)
- "But if, in our endeavor to be justified in Christ, we too were found to be sinners, is Christ then a servant of sin?" (Gal. 2:17)
- "Is the law then contrary to the promises of God?" (Gal. 3:21)[1]

The phrase μὴ γένοιτο "strongly deprecates something suggested by a previous question or assertion."[2] Wallace (482) notes that Paul's usage conveys "his repulsion at the thought that someone might infer an erroneous conclusion from the previous argument." Because the phrase includes the nonindicative negation (μή) + the optative of γίνομαι, perhaps the most literal translation is "May it never be!"

1. The phrase μὴ γένοιτο is also used by Paul in Gal. 6:14. Unlike the other uses, however, it is not in response to a rhetorical question. Luke's only use is found in Luke 20:16.
2. Ernest DeWitt Burton, *Syntax of the Moods and Tenses in New Testament Greek*, 3rd ed. (Edinburgh: T&T Clark, 1898), 79.

(NASB). Nearly every major English version, however, translates the phrase differently. The following are translations of Romans 7:7:

- "Absolutely not!" (CSB, NET)
- "By no means!" (RSV, NRSV, ESV)
- "No, not at all!" (NLV)
- "God forbid" (KJV)
- "Certainly not!" (NIV, NKJV)
- "Out of the question!" (NJB)
- "Of course not!" (NLT)

In their different ways, these translations are trying to convey the utter rejection of the thought. Most of the translations rightly include the word "not" or "no" to communicate such rejection. Other more dynamic translations—such as the KJV's "God forbid" and the NJB's "Out of the question!"—do so in a more idiomatic fashion. Another dynamic translation might be something like "Perish the thought." The KJV is probably the least helpful since some might think that the Greek actually contains the word for "God."[3]

It is also best to translate μὴ γένοιτο consistently in each of its similar uses. That is, when the phrase strongly rejects a rhetorical question, it is best to render it the same way each time so that a reader can see the parallel uses. Unfortunately, some of the English versions fail this test. For example, the ESV translates the phrase fairly consistently within each biblical book, but each book is different from the others.

- Romans (e.g., 3:31): "By no means!"
- 1 Corinthians (6:15): "Never!"
- Galatians (2:17): "Certainly not!"

In the end, there are a number of helpful ways to render μὴ γένοιτο. What is most important is that we feel the weight of such emphatic

---

3. Interestingly, Young (141) states that the translation "God forbid!" is "a rendering unsurpassed by any modern version." There is obviously doubt that such a rendering is best, especially since modern translations have not followed the KJV.

denial. So when Paul asks, "Do you not know that your bodies are members of Christ? Shall I then take the members of Christ and make them members of a prostitute?" (1 Cor. 6:15), we should feel the weight of Paul's utter rejection of such a thought. Because we have been bought with the price of Christ's death, we are no longer our own. Consequently, we have the obligation to glorify God with our bodies—which means being sexually pure. Thus the body is not insignificant in the Christian worldview since we are united with Christ.

# 21

# ADVERBIAL PARTICIPLES

## 1 Peter 5:6–7

## Introduction

Humility is an important character quality for a Christian. Conversely, pride is the source of most sins that Christians commit and therefore must be resisted. But the concept of humility is often difficult to define or describe. Precisely how do humble people act? Are they quiet, restrained, introverted, gentle, passive, and/or indecisive? For example, Peter exhorts the believers scattered in Pontus, Galatia, Cappadocia, Asia, and Bithynia: "Humble yourselves, therefore, under the mighty hand of God so that at the proper time he may exalt you" (1 Pet. 5:6). Notice that Peter commands his audience with an imperative (ταπεινώθητε). Consequently, Christians are commanded to humble themselves under God so that he can exalt them at the proper time. But precisely what does it mean for us to humble ourselves?

## Overview

Adverbial participles are grammatically subordinate to a main verb, functioning similarly to adverbs. They answer questions such as "when?" or "why?" or "how?" An adverbial participle will never be directly preceded by an article and is thus in the predicate position. It is only the lexical nature of the verb and the context that determine the particular use of each participle. That is, the grammatical form itself does not identify the usage. Rather, the adverbial force of a participle is related to the relationship between the participle, the main verb, and the context. Robertson (1124) notes, "In itself, it must be distinctly noted, the participle does not express time, manner, cause, purpose, condition or concession. These ideas are not in the participle, but are merely suggested by the context, if at all, or occasionally by a particle."[1]

- *Temporal* (the present participle portrays an action as ongoing, usually occurring simultaneously as the main verb; the aorist participle portrays the action holistically, usually occurring before the action of the main verb): "He said these things while teaching [διδάσκων] in the synagogue in Capernaum" (John 6:59 CSB).
- *Means* (answers *how* the main verb was accomplished): "Christ redeemed us from the curse of the law by becoming [γενόμενος] a curse for us" (Gal. 3:13).
- *Manner* (answers *how* the main verb was performed, often translated as an adverb): "He went away grieving [λυπούμενος]" (Matt. 19:22 CSB).
- *Cause* (answers *why* the action is accomplished, providing the reason or grounds): "We also glory in our sufferings, because we know [εἰδότες] that suffering produces perseverance" (Rom. 5:3 NIV).
- *Purpose* (indicates the *intended* purpose of the main verb's action): "He had come to Jerusalem to worship [προσκυνήσων]" (Acts 8:27).
- *Result* (indicates the *actual* result of the main's verb action): "that he might create in himself one new man in place of the two, so making [ποιῶν] peace" (Eph. 2:15).

1. See also BDF §417, p. 215; B&W 146.

- *Condition* (introduces the protasis of conditional statement): "For what does it profit a man if he gains [κερδήσας] the whole world and loses or forfeits himself" (Luke 9:25).

- *Concession* (conveys the reason an action should *not* take place, although it does): "Although they knew [γνόντες] God, they did not honor him as God" (Rom. 1:21).

## Interpretation

So how do we humble ourselves under the mighty hand of God? The following verse provides the answer: "casting [ἐπιρίψαντες] all your anxieties on him, because he cares for you" (1 Pet. 5:7). That is, the adverbial participle most likely functions as a participle of means (or instrumental participle). If that is the case, then it could be translated "by casting" all your cares on him. In fact, this is how the NET translates the verse: "by casting all your cares on him because he cares for you."

Unfortunately, some English versions translate the participle as an independent imperatival participle.

- NIV, NRSV: "Cast all your anxiety on him because he cares for you."
- RSV: "Cast all your anxieties on him, for he cares about you."
- NJB: "unload all your burden on to him, since he is concerned about you."
- NLT: "Give all your worries and cares to God, for he cares about you."

Wallace (630) rightly notes, "Although treated as an independent command in several modern translations (e.g., RSV, NRSV, NIV), the participle should be connected with the verb of verse 6, ταπεινώθητε." If the participle is adverbial (and nearly all scholars affirm that it is), then it should be interpreted as a subordinate verb related to the main verb. Wallace (630) continues, "As such, it is not offering a new command, but is defining *how* believers are to humble themselves.

Taking the participle as means enriches our understanding of both verbs: Humbling oneself is not a negative act of self-denial per se, but a positive one of active dependence on God for help."[2] Likewise, Schreiner asserts,

> The participle should be understood as an instrumental participle, and it explains *how* believers can humble themselves under God's strong hand. Seeing the relationship between the main verb ("Humble yourselves," v. 6) and the participle ("casting all your anxiety upon him," NASB) is important because it shows that giving in to worry is an example of pride. The logical relationship between the two clauses is as follows: believers humble themselves *by casting* their worries on God. Conversely, if believers continue to worry, then they are caving in to pride.[3]

In this case the syntax of the Greek text clarifies how believers are to obey God's command. The way we humble ourselves before our Maker and Creator is to cast all our cares on him. Pride says that we can do it on our own. Humility embraces the help of another who can bear our load for us.

---

2. Wayne Grudem likewise declares, "No new sentence begins here in Greek, and an important connection between verses 6 and 7 is missed by those English translations (such as RSV and NIV) which start a new sentence at verse 7. Peter continues the command of verse 6 ('Humble yourselves . . .') with a participial phrase telling how this is to be done. Proper humility is attained by 'casting all your anxieties on him, for he cares about you.'" *1 Peter,* TNTC 17 (Grand Rapids: Eerdmans, 1988), 195.

3. Thomas R. Schreiner, *1–2 Peter, Jude,* NAC 37 (Nashville: Broadman & Holman, 2003), 240. See also J. Ramsey Michaels, *1 Peter,* WBC 49 (Waco: Word, 1988), 296; Peter H. Davids, *The First Epistle of Peter,* NICNT (Grand Rapids: Eerdmans, 1990), 187.

# 22

# VERBAL PARTICIPLES

## Matthew 28:19

### Introduction

There is virtually unanimous agreement that the main command of the Great Commission is to "make disciples" (μαθητεύσατε). But how should we understand the participle πορευθέντες? Is it best translated "as you go" or as a command, "Go!" In other words, are we to understand the verse as stating that our disposition as we go about our daily routine should be to make disciples? Or is this verse stating imperatively that believers are commanded to leave their homes and go to a foreign land for the express purpose of making disciples? The answer to this question is found in how we understand the participle πορευθέντες.

### Overview

Adverbial participles are dependent participles that are subordinate to the main verb (usually an indicative, an imperative, or a subjunctive

This chapter is a summary of my essay, "Why the Great Commission Should Be Translated 'Go!' and Not 'As You Go,'" *STR* 9, no. 2 (2018): 21–32.

use of an imperative). Verbal participles, however, often function as main verbs or verbs that are coordinate with a main verb. Here are some examples of verbal participles:

- *Attendant circumstance* (parallel to the main verb, thus taking on its mood): "<u>Rise</u> [ἀναστάς] and go" (Luke 17:19).

- *Genitive absolute* (a genitive adverbial participle that provides background information): "<u>As</u> he <u>was saying</u> [λαλοῦντος] these things, many believed" (John 8:30).

- *Imperatival* (an independent participle that functions as an imperative): "<u>Rejoice</u> [χαίροντες] in hope" (Rom. 12:12).

- *Pleonastic* (a redundant expression usually employing ἀποκριθείς or λέγων): "And Jesus <u>answered</u> [ἀποκριθεὶς . . . εἶπεν] them" (Matt. 11:4).

- *Complementary* (completes the idea of the main verb): "I never <u>stop</u> [παύομαι] <u>giving thanks</u> [εὐχαριστῶν] for you" (Eph. 1:16 CSB).

- *Indirect discourse* (an anarthrous accusative participle that expresses what someone said): "those who do not confess that Jesus Christ <u>has come</u> [ἐρχόμενον] in the flesh" (2 John 7 NRSV).

The participle of attendant circumstance functions parallel with a main verb, taking on the mood of the main verb. It is typically translated as a finite verb with "and" inserted between the participle and the main verb. Wallace (642) lists five characteristics that *all* occur in at least 90 percent of participles clearly identified as attendant circumstance: (1) the tense of the participle is usually *aorist*; (2) the tense of the main verb is usually *aorist*; (3) the mood of the main verb is usually *indicative* or *imperative*; (4) the participle will *precede the main verb*; and (5) the participle occurs frequently in *historical narratives*. Although the participle and the main verb are translated as parallel or coordinate verbs, the emphasis still falls on the main verb, with the participle being grammatically subordinate.

## Interpretation

Although some maintain that the aorist participle πορευθέντες in Matthew 28:19 should be viewed as a temporal (adverbial) participle and should therefore be translated "as you go,"[1] the best evidence supports taking it as a participle of attendant circumstance. As such, the participle mirrors the main verb, which in this case is an imperative, and therefore the participle should be translated as an imperative. This use of the participle is confirmed by looking at similar constructions in both the Septuagint and the NT, especially the Gospel of Matthew.

First, there are several key texts in the Septuagint demonstrating that the participle often functions imperatively.[2]

- Rebekah tells her son Jacob, "Let your curse be on me, my son; only obey my voice, and go [πορευθείς], bring [ἔνεγκε] them to me" (Gen. 27:13). Interestingly, in the Hebrew text, both of these verbs are imperatives. Also, it would not make sense to translate the participle temporally ("as you go, bring") since it clearly bears an imperatival force ("go, bring").

- Jacob instructs his son Joseph, "Go [πορευθείς] now, see [ἰδέ] if it is well with your brothers and with the flock, and bring me word" (Gen. 37:14). As with the previous example, the Hebrew has an imperative that the Septuagint renders as a participle.

- Pharaoh commands the people of Israel, "Go [πορευθέντες] now and work [ἐργάζεσθε]. No straw will be given you, but you must still deliver the same number of bricks" (Exod. 5:18).

- After the tenth plague (the death of the firstborn), Pharaoh orders Moses and Aaron, "Take [ἀναλαβόντες] your flocks and your herds . . . and be gone [πορεύεσθε]" (Exod. 12:32).

- The sons of the prophets say to Elisha concerning Elijah, "Please let them go [πορευθέντες] and seek [ζητησάτωσαν] your master" (2 Kings 2:16).[3]

1. See, e.g., the ISV: "Therefore, as you go, disciple people in all nations, baptizing them in the name of the Father, and the Son, and the Holy Spirit."
2. See Cleon Rogers, "The Great Commission," BSac 130 (1973): 260.
3. The Hebrew verb that lies behind the Greek is a jussive with an imperatival force. See also 1 Macc. 7:7, πορευθεὶς ἰδέτω.

These texts confirm the use of the participle that functions imperatively.[4] Other uses in Matthew's Gospel also confirm the attendant circumstance use of the participle. Not only does Matthew use this construction often, but he also uses the construction with the same verb (πορεύομαι) as an aorist participle, followed by an aorist imperative.

- King Herod urgently commands the wise men, "Go [πορευθέντες] and search [ἐξετάσατε] diligently for the child" (2:8).
- Jesus states, "Go [πορευθέντες] and learn [μάθετε] what this means" (9:13).
- Jesus tells John's disciples, "Go [πορευθέντες] and tell [ἀπαγγείλατε] John what you hear and see" (11:4).
- Jesus instructs Peter, "Go [πορευθείς] to the sea and cast [βάλε] a hook and take the first fish that comes up" (17:27).
- The angel at the empty tomb tells the women, "Then go [πορευθεῖσαι] quickly and tell [εἴπατε] his disciples that he has risen from the dead" (28:7).[5]

Instead of using two coordinate imperatives, it was common to use a participle followed by an imperative. It was understood that the participle mirrored the mood of the imperative, being taken as a command.[6] In each case, it would not make much sense to translate the participle as "when/as you go," for the participle clearly functions as an imperative. Therefore, when we come to Matthew 28:19 ("Go [πορευθέντες] therefore and make disciples [μαθητεύσατε] of all nations"), it is natural to read the participle as an imperative. In Matthew's Gospel, every instance of the aorist participle of πορεύομαι preceding an aorist main verb is clearly attendant circumstance. This

4. The use of the participle as attendant circumstance should not be confused with the imperatival participle, which is very rare and is used in a construction that lacks a main verb. It is mostly found in Rom. 12 and 1 Peter.
5. For more uses of the participle of attendant circumstance in construction with imperatives, see Matt. 2:13, 20; 5:24; 9:6; 21:2.
6. In the cases where the participle indicates a temporal function, the present participle is used: Matt. 10:7; 11:7; 28:11.

interpretation is also confirmed by English Bible versions, which consistently translate πορευθέντες as an imperative. So while we acknowledge that the participle πορευθέντες is not the main verb (and thus not the main command) in the Great Commission, without doubt it carries an imperatival force ("Go!"). Consequently, the church is given a command to go to the nations in order to make disciples.

# 23

# PERIPHRASTIC
# PARTICIPLES

## Matthew 18:18

## Introduction

In both Matthew 16 and Matthew 18, Jesus offers instruction to his disciples that include a reference to something being bound and loosed.

Whatever [ὃ ἐάν] you bind [δήσῃς] on earth shall have been bound [ἔσται δεδεμένον] in heaven [τοῖς οὐρανοῖς], and whatever [ὃ ἐάν] you loose [λύσῃς] on earth shall have been loosed [ἔσται λελυμένον] in heaven [τοῖς οὐρανοῖς]. (Matt. 16:19 NASB)

Whatever [ὅσα ἐάν] you bind [δήσητε] on earth shall have been bound [ἔσται δεδεμένα] in heaven [οὐρανῷ]; and whatever [ὅσα ἐάν] you loose [λύσητε] on earth shall have been loosed [ἔσται λελυμένα] in heaven [οὐρανῷ]. (Matt. 18:18 NASB)

There are, however, some notable differences between these two passages, though most of the differences cannot be seen in the English versions:

1. "Whatever" in Matthew 16 translates a singular relative pronoun (ὅ) + ἐάν, whereas Matthew 18 has a plural correlative pronoun (ὅσα) + ἐάν.

2. The subjunctive verbs in Matthew 16 are second-person *singular* (δήσῃς, λύσῃς), whereas in Matthew 18 they are second-person *plural* (δήσητε, λύσητε).

3. "Heaven" is plural (and articular) in Matthew 16 (τοῖς οὐρανοῖς) but singular in Matthew 18 (οὐρανῷ).

4. In Matthew 16 the periphrastic participles are singular (δεδεμένον, λελυμένον), whereas in Matthew 18 they are plural (δεδεμένα, λελυμένα).

In this chapter we will focus on the meaning of the verse in Matthew 18 as it relates to the church. Exactly what does Jesus mean when he states that whatever the church binds or looses "shall have been bound" or "shall have been loosed" in heaven? Do the periphrastic constructions help settle the debate?

## Overview

The term *periphrastic* comes from the Greek περί (around) and φράζω (I explain) and refers to the roundabout way of expressing the verbal idea. Thus a periphrastic construction includes the verb εἰμί plus a participle. Instead of using one verb to express the action (ἔλεγεν = he was speaking), a verb plus a participle is used (ἦν λέγων = he was speaking). Some common characteristics of periphrastic constructions include the following: (1) the finite verb is usually εἰμί (though γίνομαι is sometimes used),[1] which can occur in the present, imperfect, or future tense-forms; (2) the participle can be either present or perfect,[2] will usually occur in the nominative case, and usually follows the indicative verb; (3) it is most common in Luke's writings,[3]

1. See Mark 9:3; 2 Cor. 6:14; Col. 1:18; Heb. 5:12; Rev. 3:2; 16:10.
2. Only two of the 270 periphrastic constructions in the NT include aorist participles: Luke 23:19; 2 Cor. 5:19.
3. More than half of the NT periphrastic constructions occur in Luke and Acts; see BDF §353, p. 179; Zerwick, *Bib. Gk.*, §361, pp. 125–26.

with the imperfect being the most common form; and (4) it is often used to highlight verbal aspect.[4] There are six different periphrastic constructions.

- *Present periphrastic* (εἰμί [pres.] + present ptc.): "They will name him Immanuel, which is translated [ἐστιν μεθερμηνευόμενον] 'God is with us'" (Matt. 1:23 CSB).
- *Imperfect periphrastic* (ἤμην [impf.] + present ptc.): "Pharisees and teachers of the law were sitting [ἦσαν καθήμενοι] there" (Luke 5:17).
- *Future periphrastic* (ἔσομαι [fut.] + present ptc.): "The stars will be falling [ἔσονται ... πίπτοντες] from heaven" (Mark 13:25).
- *Perfect periphrastic* (εἰμί [pres.] + perfect ptc.): "For nothing is covered [ἐστιν κεκαλυμμένον] that will not be revealed" (Matt. 10:26).
- *Pluperfect periphrastic* (ἤμην [impf.] + perfect ptc.): "For John had not yet been put [ἦν βεβλημένος] in prison" (John 3:24).
- *Future perfect periphrastic* (ἔσομαι [fut.] + perfect ptc.): "I will put my trust [ἔσομαι πεποιθώς] in him" (Heb. 2:13).

## Interpretation

So, what is the meaning of the future perfects in Matthew 18:18? If the construction is translated "will/shall be bound, . . . will/shall be loosed" (RSV, NRSV, ESV, KJV, NKJV, NJB, NIV, NLT), then it means that the decision of the church will later be ratified in heaven.[5] In other words, whatever the church decides, God will ratify. But if it is translated "will/shall have been bound, . . . will/shall have been

4. BDF §352, p. 179; Porter, *Idioms*, 46; M&E 225; Young 161.
5. So H. J. Cadbury, "The Meaning of John 20:23, Matthew 16:19, and Matthew 18:18," *JBL* 58 (1939): 251–54; David L. Turner, *Matthew*, BECNT (Grand Rapids: Baker Academic, 2008), 405; W. D. Davies and Dale C. Allison, *A Critical and Exegetical Commentary on the Gospel according to Matthew*, ICC, 3 vols. (Edinburgh: T&T Clark, 1991), 2:638–39.

loosed" (NASB, NET, CSB), then heaven's prior decision is later ratified by the church.[6] In other words, the church will ratify what has already been decided by God.

Porter suggests a third option, based on his theory regarding verbal aspect.[7] He concludes that the periphrastic construction is merely stative, carrying no temporal significance whatsoever: "will be in a state of boundedness/loosedness." In this case, the meaning is simply that the church's decision is in accordance with God's will, not specifying which action precedes the other.[8]

Although the third option is slightly better than the first, it seems that the second option is best. Carson ("Matthew," 424) rightly notes that "it is difficult to see why Matthew did not use either the future or the present participle in a periphrastic future if he was merely trying to denote expectation of what is to be." Similarly, France concludes that it would have been more natural for Matthew to use the simple future passive if he simply meant "will be bound/loosed."[9]

Some also have noted theological issues with the first option. For example, Morris (*Matthew*, 469) writes, "Jesus is not giving the church the right to make decisions that will then become binding on God. Such a thought is alien from anything in his teaching. He is saying that as the church is responsive to the guidance of God, it

6. So J. R. Mantey, "The Mistranslation of the Perfect Tense in John 20:23, Mt 16:19, and Mt 18.18," *JBL* 58, no. 3 (1939): 243–49; Mantey, "Distorted Translations in John 20:23; Matthew 16:18–19," *RevExp* 78 (1981): 409–16; Mantey, "Evidence That the Perfect Tense in John 20:23 and Matthew 16:19 Is Mistranslated," *JETS* 16 (1973): 129–38; J. Marcus, "The Gates of Hades and the Keys of the Kingdom (Matt 16:18–19)," *CBQ* 50 (1988): 443–55; Leon Morris, *The Gospel according to Matthew*, PNTC (Grand Rapids: Eerdmans, 1992), 426, 469; R. T. France, *The Gospel of Matthew*, NICNT (Grand Rapids: Eerdmans, 2007), 626–27, 697; France, *Matthew: Evangelist and Teacher* (Grand Rapids: Zondervan, 1989), 247n11; Craig S. Keener, *The Gospel of Matthew: A Socio-Rhetorical Commentary* (Grand Rapids: Eerdmans, 2009), 454–55; D. A. Carson, "Matthew," in *The Expositor's Bible Commentary*, ed. Tremper Longman III and David E. Garland, rev. ed. (Grand Rapids: Zondervan, 2010), 9:421–24.

7. Stanley E. Porter, "Vague Verbs, Periphrastics, and Matt. 16.19," *Filología Neotestamentaria* 1 (1988): 155–73.

8. So M&E 224–25; Craig L. Blomberg, *Matthew*, NAC 22 (Nashville: Broadman & Holman, 1992), 255; Grant R. Osborne, *Matthew*, ZECNT (Grand Rapids: Zondervan, 2010), 628–29.

9. France, *Matthew*, 627. But cf. Isa. 8:17; Luke 12:52; Heb. 2:13.

will come to the decisions that have already been made in heaven." Morris (*Matthew*, 469) continues by adding that such decisions can be "made in the light of the guidance of the Spirit of God" (cf. John 20:22–23). In a similar vein, France asserts, "In this syntactical form the saying becomes a promise not of divine *endorsement*, but of divine *guidance* to enable Peter [and the church] to decide in accordance with God's already determined purpose."[10]

Perhaps there is an analogy between the church discipline case found in 1 Corinthians 5 with what we find here in Matthew 18. If the second view is correct, then the church is to ratify the previous decision made in heaven by God. Similarly, in 1 Corinthians 5:3, Paul states, "For though absent in body, I am present in spirit; and as if present, I have already pronounced judgment on the one who did such a thing." That is, the church is called to exercise its authority regarding the expelling of an immoral "brother" since Paul himself has already passed judgment on the case. In other words, it is God's will that the local church discipline those who are unrepentant, and when such discipline takes place, the church can be assured that their decision is in line with God's will. Thus these verses grant confidence and assurance to the church, so that they can be confident of doing God's will in enforcing church discipline. Whenever such decisions are made, the church can be assured that what they do on earth accords with God's will in heaven. The church's binding and loosing is only authoritative when it corresponds with the divine will.

---

10. France, *Matthew*, 627. Likewise, Osborne (*Matthew*, 629) declares, "Surely this cannot be correct, as if God is bound to accept the church's decisions."

# 24

# INFINITIVES

## 1 Timothy 6:17–18

### Introduction

Being rich can be scary if you read the Bible. Jesus himself declares, "It is easier for a camel to go through the eye of a needle than for a rich person to enter the kingdom of God" (Matt. 19:24; see also Mark 10:25; Luke 18:25). Paul likewise warns about the dangers of the love of money and warns his spiritual son Timothy to flee from wealth's temptations (1 Tim. 6:10). Using five infinitives, Paul later instructs Timothy to pass along an admonition specifically for the rich: "As for the rich in this present age, charge them not to be haughty [ὑψηλοφρονεῖν], nor to set their hopes [ἠλπικέναι] on the uncertainty of riches, but on God, who richly provides us with everything to enjoy. They are to do good [ἀγαθοεργεῖν], to be rich [πλουτεῖν] in good works, to be [εἶναι] generous and ready to share" (1 Tim. 6:17–18). Why does Paul single out the rich here, and how does understanding the infinitives help us grasp the meaning of this admonition?

## Overview

An infinitive is a verbal noun. As such, it has both verbal qualities and noun qualities. Like a verb, an infinitive has aspect and voice and can take a direct object or be modified by an adverb. The subject of the infinitive occurs in the accusative case (instead of the nominative case), and the infinitive is negated by μή. An infinitive is indeclinable, not having person and number. Like a noun, an infinitive can take an article (which is always neuter and singular: τό, τοῦ, and τῷ) and can have a variety of different case functions. When occurring after a preposition in the NT, the infinitive is always articular and functions adverbially. Infinitives are quite frequent in the NT, occurring 2,291 times (more than 86 percent are anarthrous). Adverbial infinitives include the following:

- *Complementary* (completes the idea of another verb): "Who can [δύναται] forgive [ἀφιέναι] sins but God alone?" (Mark 2:7).

- *Purpose* (communicates the goal expressed by the main verb): "Two men went up into the temple to pray [προσεύξασθαι]" (Luke 18:10).

- *Result* (communicates the actual or conceived result expressed by the main verb): "Therefore do not let sin reign in your mortal body, so that you obey [εἰς τὸ ὑπακούειν] its desires" (Rom. 6:12 CSB).

- *Previous time* (the action of the infinitive occurs *before* the main verb: μετὰ τό + inf.): "But after I am raised up [μετὰ τὸ ἐγερθῆναι], I will go before you to Galilee" (Matt. 26:32).

- *Contemporaneous time* (the action of the infinitive occurs *simultaneously* with the main verb: ἐν τῷ + inf.): "While they were traveling [ἐν τῷ πορεύεσθαι], he entered a village" (Luke 10:38 CSB).

- *Subsequent time* (the action of the infinitive occurs *after* the main verb: πρὸ τοῦ or πρίν [ἤ] + inf.): "I am telling you this now, before it takes place [πρὸ τοῦ γενέσθαι]" (John 13:19).

- *Cause* (communicates the reason for the action of the main verb: διὰ τό + inf.): "He holds his priesthood permanently, because he continues [διὰ τὸ μένειν] forever" (Heb. 7:24).

- *Means* (conveys the means by which the action of the main verb is performed: ἐν τῷ + inf.): "Grant to Your servants that with all boldness they may speak Your word, by stretching [ἐν τῷ ἐκτείνειν] out Your hand" (Acts 4:29–30 NKJV).

Unlike adverbial infinitives that are syntactically linked to verbs, substantival infinitives function as nouns or other substantives.

- *Subject* (functions as the subject or predicate nominative of a main verb): "To write [γράφειν] the same things to you is no trouble to me" (Phil. 3:1).

- *Direct object* (functions as the direct object of a main verb): "I do not refuse to die [τὸ ἀποθανεῖν]" (Acts 25:11 NASB).

- *Indirect discourse* (follows a verb of speaking to communicate indirect speech): "I therefore . . . urge [παρακαλῶ] you to walk [περιπατῆσαι] in a manner worthy of the calling to which you have been called" (Eph. 4:1).

- *Explanatory* (defines or clarifies a noun or adjective): "For this is the will of God, your sanctification: that you abstain [ἀπέχεσθαι] from sexual immorality" (1 Thess. 4:3).

We will also list a few uses of the infinitive that function independently of a main verb, either functioning as an imperative (imperatival) or unrelated to any verb (absolute).

- *Imperatival* (functions as an imperative, lacking a main verb in context): "Weep [κλαίειν] with those who weep" (Rom. 12:15).

- *Absolute* (functions independently of the rest of the sentence): "Claudius Lysias, to his Excellency the governor Felix, greetings [χαίρειν]" (Acts 23:26).

## Interpretation

In 1 Timothy 6:17–18 the particular construction that Paul uses to convey his message to the rich is a series of infinitives of indirect discourse.

Such infinitives follow a verb of speech (such as παραγγέλλω) and function similar to an imperative. Using this construction to charge the rich not to be haughty is similar to Timothy actually charging them, "Don't be haughty." The former is indirect discourse, and the latter is direct discourse. Why does Paul single out the rich? First, earlier in the epistle we learn that the false teachers are captivated by money (3:3, 8). Thus he exhorts the congregation and Timothy to be content with what they have and to avoid the dangerous trap of "the love of money" (6:10). Second, Paul realizes that money is a danger not only for false teachers but also for all believers. Chrysostom rightly says, "And this advice he gives, knowing that nothing so generally produces pride and arrogance as wealth."[1]

In order to convey his message, Paul strings together a series of five infinitives in 1 Timothy 6:17–18 to charge the rich:

1. "not to be haughty [ὑψηλοφρονεῖν]"
2. "nor to set their hopes [ἠλπικέναι] on the uncertainty of riches, but on God"
3. "to do good [ἀγαθοεργεῖν]"
4. "to be rich [πλουτεῖν] in good works"
5. "to be [εἶναι] generous and ready to share"

The first infinitive, ὑψηλοφρονεῖν, is a compound of ὑψηλός (high, lofty) and φρονέω (to think). This is the only occurrence in the NT, but a similar form is found in Romans 11:20, where Paul warns the Gentiles, "Do not become proud [μὴ ὑψηλὰ φρόνει], but fear."[2] Later he exhorts, "Do not be haughty [μὴ τὰ ὑψηλὰ φρονοῦντες], but associate with the lowly" (Rom. 12:16). The rich must not let their riches puff them up with pride since everything they have is a gift from God. Consequently, they are not to set their hope on their wealth. The second infinitive, ἠλπικέναι, is a perfect tense-form stressing the present state of Paul's injunction. Riches are not a good foundation for one's

---

1. "Homily 18 on 1 Timothy," in NPNF[1] 13:472, quoted in William D. Mounce, *Pastoral Epistles*, WBC 46 (Nashville: Nelson, 2000), 366.
2. The textual variant ὑψηλὰ φρονεῖν in 1 Tim. 6:17 demonstrates that the non-compound form was virtually equivalent; BDF §119.5, p. 65.

hope, since they are so uncertain (Pss. 52:7; 62:10; Prov. 23:4–5; Jer. 9:23; Luke 12:16–21). Instead, believers are to set their hope on the unchanging God, who abundantly provides for his children. The third infinitive, ἀγαθοεργεῖν, is a compound of ἀγαθός (good) and ἐργάζομαι (to work).[3] Those who realize that "every good and perfect gift" comes "from above" (James 1:17) will respond by helping others. The fourth infinitive, πλουτεῖν (to be rich), is the last word involving a wordplay on the theme of "rich" (πλούσιος): "As for the rich [πλουσίοις] in this present age, charge them not to be haughty, nor to set their hopes on the uncertainty of riches [πλούτου], but on God, who richly [πλουσίως] provides us with everything to enjoy. They are to do good, to be rich [πλουτεῖν] in good works, to be generous and ready to share" (1 Tim. 6:17–18).[4] The final infinitive, εἶναι, is linked with εὐμεταδότους (generous) and κοινωνικούς (ready to share) and in the context refers to sharing material goods with those in need (cf. Rom. 12:8, 13; 2 Cor. 9:11–13). Those who are rich have the responsibility to view their wealth in a way that keeps them humble, allowing them to be generous, ready and willing to share with others. In doing this, they provide for themselves a treasure in heaven "where neither moth nor rust destroys and where thieves do not break in and steal" (Matt. 6:20).

3. For the only other occurrence of the word in the NT, see Acts 14:17, where it is used of God.
4. Paul continues the theme in 1 Tim. 6:19 by adding that those who follow his advice are "storing up treasure [ἀποθησαυρίζοντας] for themselves" (ESV) "in the life to come" (Phillips).

# 25

# PRONOUNS

## Luke 16:19–20

### Introduction

Is the story of the rich man and Lazarus a real-life story or a made-up parable? In Luke 16:19–20 we read, "There was a *rich man* who would dress in purple and fine linen, feasting lavishly every day. But a poor man named *Lazarus*, covered with sores, was lying at his gate" (CSB, emphasis added). Some claim that this is a real-life story that should be interpreted literally. Others claim that this is a parable and therefore the details of the story should not be pressed. Which is correct? Thankfully, the Greek text offers us clues as to which option is best.

### Overview

A pronoun takes the place of a noun. The noun that the pronoun replaces is called the antecedent. There are at least eight types of pronouns found in the Greek of the NT (see the table).

The indefinite pronoun τις (anyone) is normally somewhat insignificant. It is typically used when an individual (anyone) or group (certain ones) is not named or is unknown and often appears in combination with the subjunctive mood, which communicates something that is probable or indefinite. Careful attention to the indefinite pronoun, however, can sometimes lead to a proper understanding of a text.

| Personal | ἐγώ, ἐμοῦ/μου, σύ, ὑμῶν, αὐτοῦ | I, my, you, your [pl.], his |
|---|---|---|
| Demonstrative | Near οὗτος, οὗτοι | this, these |
| | Far ἐκεῖνος, ἐκεῖνοι | that, those |
| Relative | ὅς(τις), ἧς, ὅ | who, whose, which |
| Interrogative | τίς, τίνος, τί | who? whose? what/why? |
| Indefinite | τις, τινες | anyone/someone, certain ones |
| Reflexive | ἐμαυτόν, ἑαυτούς, ἑαυτοῖς | myself, yourselves, to themselves |
| Reciprocal | ἀλλήλων | [of] one another |
| Correlative | ὅσος, οἷος, ὁποῖος | as many as, such as, what sort of |

## Interpretation

As mentioned above, many interpret the story of the rich man and Lazarus as a real-life story, which therefore should be interpreted literally.[1] That is, what Jesus proclaims is not a story invented to teach a moral lesson but something that actually happened. There are two main reasons for this interpretation. (1) The Gospel writers normally introduce the parables of Jesus with a phrase such as "He told them a parable" (e.g., Luke 18:1, 9), and this story contains no such introduction. (2) Jesus never gives actual names of characters in his parables, but in this story he identifies one character as "Lazarus." In other words, if this story is a parable, it would be the only parable in which an individual is named. This was the position of John Wesley, who stated the following in one of his sermons:

1. For example, Elmer L. Towns and Ben Gutiérrez state: "The story of the rich man and Lazarus is sometimes thought to be a parable (16:19–31). However, this is a true story about two individuals." *The Essence of the New Testament* (Nashville: B&H, 2012), 86. See also R. Summers, *Commentary on Luke* (Waco: Word, 1972), 194; James A. Borland, "Luke," in *Liberty Bible Commentary*, ed. Jerry Falwell, Edward E. Hindson, and Woodrow Michael Kroll (Lynchburg, VA: Old-Time Gospel Hour, 1982), 185–86.

## CHAPTER 25

But is the subsequent account merely a parable, or a real history? It has been believed by many, and roundly asserted, to be a mere parable, because of one or two circumstances therein, which are not easy to be accounted for. In particular, it is hard to conceive, how a person in hell could hold conversation with one in paradise. But, admitting we cannot account for this, will it overbalance an express assertion of our Lord: "There was," says our Lord, "a certain rich man."— Was there not? Did such a man never exist? "And there was a certain beggar named Lazarus."—Was there, or was there not? Is it not bold enough, positively to deny what our blessed Lord positively affirms? Therefore, we cannot reasonably doubt, but the whole narration, with all its circumstances, is exactly true.[2]

However, the reasons offered as to why this story must be interpreted as a real-life event are weak. (1) The Gospel writers do not always indicate if a story is a parable. For example, although virtually all scholars agree that the story of the dishonest manager (or the shrewd steward) is a parable, Luke does not explicitly indicate that it is a parable: "He also said to the disciples, 'There was a rich man who had a manager'" (16:1). (2) Although it is true that Jesus does not use proper names elsewhere in his parables, he does often use details to make a parable appear to be more true to life. Also, the name "Lazarus" (from Eleazer) may be significant because it means "God has helped." Though other people may not have helped him, God did.[3] Yet the most important feature in determining whether this story is a parable is Luke's use of the indefinite pronoun τις.

Seven times Luke begins a parable with the phrase "[There was] a certain [τις] man [ἄνθρωπος]" (NKJV).[4]

---

2. John Wesley, "Sermon 112," preached in Birmingham, March 25, 1788, in *The Works of John Wesley*, 3rd ed. (Peabody, MA: Hendrickson, 1984), 7:245.

3. See Robert H. Stein, *Luke*, NAC 24 (Nashville: Broadman, 1992), 421–22; David E. Garland, *Luke*, ZECNT (Grand Rapids: Zondervan, 201), 669. Walter L. Liefeld and David W. Pao comment that the name *Lazarus* "is probably used symbolically" to mean "the one who received no help from those around him receives deliverance from God in heaven." "Luke," in *The Expositor's Bible Commentary*, ed. Tremper Longman III and David E. Garland, rev. ed. (Grand Rapids: Zondervan, 2007), 10:264.

4. Unfortunately, this stylized introduction is often obscured by modern English versions. The verses are cited from the NKJV, which best illustrates our point.

- "A <u>certain man</u> [ἄνθρωπός τις] went down from Jerusalem to Jericho" (10:30).
- "A <u>certain man</u> [ἄνθρωπός τις] gave a great supper and invited many" (14:16).
- "A <u>certain man</u> [ἄνθρωπός τις] had two sons" (15:11).
- "There was a <u>certain</u> rich <u>man</u> [ἄνθρωπός τις] who had a steward" (16:1).
- "A <u>certain noble</u><u>man</u> [ἄνθρωπός τις] went into a far country to receive for himself a kingdom, and to return" (19:12).
- "A <u>certain man</u> [ἄνθρωπός (τις)] planted a vineyard" (20:9).[5]

So we should not be surprised when we find the same pattern in Luke 16:19: "There was a <u>certain</u> rich <u>man</u> [ἄνθρωπος τις] who was clothed in purple and fine linen and who feasted sumptuously every day." Luke uses the same introduction in 16:1, "There was a certain rich man." By using this pattern, Luke is signaling to his readers that Jesus is telling another parable. Consequently, the story should be interpreted as a parable and not as a historical narrative. Of course, the fact that it is a parable does not make it any less valuable or authoritative. It does, however, mean that we employ the appropriate hermeneutical principles so as not to distort the original intention of the author.

5. See also Luke 7:41, "There was a <u>certain</u> [τινι] creditor who had two debtors" (NKJV); and 18:2, "A <u>certain</u> [τις] judge was in a <u>certain</u> [τινι] city" (trans. author). There is only one example of Luke using ἄνθρωπός τις that is not in the context of a parable: 14:2, "And behold, there was a <u>certain man</u> [ἄνθρωπός τις] before Him who had dropsy" (NKJV). The difference between this example and the other seven uses is that the parables are always introduced with "He [Jesus] was saying/said," whereas 14:2 is clearly part of a narrative.

# 26

# PREPOSITIONS

## Ephesians 4:12

### Introduction

Prepositions sometimes feel like small words that just get in the way of real exegesis and Bible exposition. But we must be careful here because the relationship of a prepositional phrase to the rest of the sentence can alter one's interpretation of a passage. For example, in Ephesians 1:4, does "in love" (ἐν ἀγάπῃ) modify the previous phrase ("that we should be holy and blameless before him in love")[1] or the following phrase ("in love he predestined us")?[2] Similarly, in Ephesians 4:12, Paul uses three prepositional phrases in explaining why Christ gave leaders to the church:

<u>to</u> [πρός] equip the saints

<u>for</u> [εἰς] the work of ministry

<u>for</u> [εἰς] building up the body of Christ.

1. So UBS[5], NA[28], CSB, NKJV, and NRSV.
2. So ESV, NASB, and NIV. This view is more likely because the focus of the benediction is on God's work of blessing his people. Additionally, if the prepositional phrase modified ἁγίους and ἀμώμους, then it should directly follow those adjectives instead of κατενώπιον αὐτοῦ. Finally, there is no example in Paul's writings of ἐν ἀγάπῃ modifying ἁγίους καὶ ἀμώμους.

But precisely how do these prepositional phrases relate to one another? Are they three parallel or coordinate prepositional phrases, as suggested by the KJV: "For the perfecting of the saints, for the work of the ministry, for the edifying of the body of Christ"? Or are the second two phrases subordinate to the first (most English versions)? And what is the significance of such an apparently minor difference?

## Overview

Prepositions help substantives express their relationship with other components of the sentence. The preposition, along with its object, constitutes a prepositional phrase. Consequently, it is necessary to consider how the entire prepositional phrase relates to the rest of the sentence. Prepositional phrases can function adverbially (modifying a verb) and adjectivally (modifying a noun or other substantive). Adverbial prepositional phrases are the most common and answer questions related to the verbal action such as "when?" "where?" "why?" or "how?" Adjectival prepositional phrases modify an explicit noun (or other substantive), answering questions such as "which?" or "what kind of"? A prepositional phrase can be substantized by placing an article in front of it, causing the phrase to function as a virtual noun (e.g., "the things in the world," τὰ ἐν τῷ κόσμῳ, 1 John 2:15).

Prepositions can be divided into proper and improper prepositions. Proper prepositions are those that occur in prepositional phrases (e.g., ἐκ πνεύματος ἁγίου, Matt. 1:18) *and* as prefixes forming compound verbs (e.g., ἐκπορεύομαι). There are four possible effects that the preposition can have on a verb when a preposition is prefixed to form a compound verb (see KMP 400): (1) additional meaning (e.g., ἀναβαίνω, I go up); (2) intensive meaning (e.g., κατεσθίω, I devour); (3) no added meaning (e.g., ἀνοίγω, I open); or (4) unrelated meaning (e.g., ἀναγινώσκω, I read). There are seventeen proper prepositions in the Greek NT.[3] Improper prepositions are prepositions that are

---

3. Proper prepositions: ἀνά, ἀντί, ἀπό, διά, εἰς, ἐκ, ἐν, ἐπί, κατά, μετά, παρά, περί, πρό, πρός, σύν, ὑπέρ, and ὑπό. For an excellent work on prepositions, see Murray J. Harris, *Prepositions and Theology in the Greek New Testament* (Grand Rapids: Zondervan, 2012).

*never* prefixed to a verb to create a compound verb (e.g., ἕως). There are forty-two improper prepositions in the Greek NT.

## Interpretation

In Ephesians 4:11–12 Paul indicates that Christ has given leaders (apostles, prophets, evangelists, and pastor-teachers) to the church for a particular reason: they are given "to [πρός] equip the saints for [εἰς] the work of ministry, for [εἰς] building up the body of Christ." The key issue before us is how these prepositional phrases relate to one another. In particular, what is the relationship of the second phrase to the first? Is it coordinate or subordinate?[4]

Some maintain that the second phrase "for [εἰς] the work of ministry" (along with the third) is coordinate (parallel) to the previous phrase "to [πρός] equip the saints." If that is the case, then the three prepositional phrases convey the purpose for which Christ gave church leaders. That is, they are given (1) to equip the saints, (2) to do the work of the ministry, and (3) to build up the body of Christ. Notice that it is the leaders who do the work of the ministry and not the equipped saints. The KJV favors this interpretation by placing a comma after the first purpose statement, indicating a parallel structure. This view "portrays the gifted people in verse 11 as the ones referred to in all the above three phrases with the rest of the people having little responsibility, thereby making a definite distinction between the clergy and laity."[5] The following arguments are often offered in support of this view: (1) it is an ancient view going back at least as far as Chrysostom;[6] (2) the author of Ephesians often strings together coordinate prepositional phrases (e.g., 1:3; 1:5–6, 20–21; 2:7; 4:13–14; 6:12); (3) it makes the best sense of the term διακονία (ministry); and (4) it fits in the immediate context of 4:11, which focuses on Christ's giving of ministers.

However, the view that the second prepositional phrase is subordinate to the first phrase is more likely correct. On this reading, Paul

4. The following discussion is summarized in Benjamin L. Merkle, *Ephesians*, EGGNT (Nashville: B&H, 2016), 128–29.
5. Harold W. Hoehner, *Ephesians: An Exegetical Commentary* (Grand Rapids: Baker Academic, 2002), 547.
6. "Homily 11 on Ephesians," in *NPNF*[1] 13:104–5.

is not providing parallel statements; rather, the second prepositional phrase provides the goal of the first prepositional phrase. That is, Christ's purpose in giving leaders to the church is so that they will equip the saints to do the work of ministry. This view is favored by nearly every English Bible version as well as many commentators.[7] Supporting such an interpretation are (1) the change in prepositions from πρός to εἰς,[8] (2) the presence of the article before the object of the first preposition but not before the object of the next two prepositions, (3) the location of τῶν ἁγίων after πρὸς τὸν καταρτισμόν instead of at the end of the verse, and (4) the emphasis on gifts given to "to each one" (ἑνὶ ἑκάστῳ, 4:7) so that "each part" (ἑνὸς ἑκάστου μέρους, 4:16) does its work (cf. 1 Cor. 12:7). Hoehner (*Ephesians*, 549) summarizes, "The point is that the gifted persons listed in verse 11 serve as the foundational gifts that are used for the immediate purpose of preparing all the saints to minister. Thus, every believer must do the work of the ministry." Arnold (*Ephesians*, 262) states his view even more forcefully: "Christ has given gifted leaders to the church not merely to do the ministry, but to invest their time heavily in developing and preparing fellow believers to engage in ministry to the body. The model Paul presents is therefore one of mutual service in the community and not one of professionals serving a group of consumers."

---

7. See, e.g., Clinton E. Arnold, *Ephesians*, ZECNT (Grand Rapids: Zondervan, 2010), 262–64; Ernest Best, *Ephesians*, ICC (London: T&T Clark, 1998), 397–99; F. F. Bruce, *The Epistles to the Colossians, to Philemon, and to the Ephesians*, NICNT (Grand Rapids: Eerdmans, 1984), 349; Hoehner, *Ephesians*, 547–49; Mark D. Roberts, *Ephesians*, Story of God Bible Commentary (Grand Rapids: Zondervan, 2016), 134–35; Klyne Snodgrass, *Ephesians*, NIVAC (Grand Rapids: Zondervan, 1996), 204; Frank Thielman, *Ephesians*, BECNT (Grand Rapids: Baker Academic, 2010), 278–80.

8. Best (*Ephesians*, 398) notes, "The change in preposition between 12a and 12bc confirms that the movement from the discussion of the work of ministers (v. 11) to that of the whole church takes place between 12a and 12bc." Although this particular series of prepositions occurs nowhere else in the NT, Arnold (*Ephesians*, 262) maintains that in the Septuagint (LXX Gen. 32:3 [32:4 Eng.]; 35:27; Josh. 9:6; 10:6; Jer. 40:12 [47:12 Eng.]) "the first prepositional phrase (πρός) is not coordinate with the other two phrases (headed by εἰς)."

# 27

## ADVERBS

### Romans 11:26

**Introduction**

Just because something is well known doesn't mean it is correctly understood. John 3:16 is the most well-known verse in the Bible, but some of the details may not be appropriately acknowledged. For example, when the verse states that "God so loved the world," the word translated "so" (οὕτως) means "in this manner" or "thus" and not "so much." The manner comes in the following phrase. *In what way* did God love the world? Answer: he gave his only Son. The NJB captures this nicely: "For this is how God loved the world: he gave his only Son."

The same adverb (οὕτως) is also found in another well-known, but also highly disputed, passage. In Romans 11:26 we read: "And in this way [οὕτως] all Israel will be saved." Much of the debate regarding this passage and the future of ethnic Israel revolves around the adverb οὕτως. What are the options, and what difference does it make?

## Overview

An adverb modifies a verb (or an adjective or another adverb). Samuel Lamerson defines an adverb as "a word that describes a verb or tells how the action was accomplished."[1] For example, "She was reading *quietly.*" Typically adverbs are not inflected but rather maintain a fixed form. The most common endings for an adverb are -ως or -ον. Adverbs answer questions related to how the action of the verb was performed, questions such as "when?" "where?" "in what way?" and "how often/intensely?" Other parts of speech can also function as adverbs, such as prepositional phrases, participles, and infinitives.

- *Adverbs of time*: ἅπαξ (once, 11× in the NT), αὔριον (tomorrow, 14×), νῦν (now, 147×), πάλιν (again, 141×), πάντοτε (always, 41×), ποτέ (formerly, 29×), πότε (when? 19×), πρωΐ (early, 12×), σήμερον (today, 41×), τότε (then, 160×).

- *Adverbs of place*: ἄνω (above, 9×), ἄνωθεν (from above, 13×), ἐκεῖ (there, 95×), ἐκεῖθεν (from there, 27×), κάτω (down, 9×), κύκλῳ (around, 8×), ποῦ (where? 52×), ὧδε (here, 61×).

- *Adverbs of manner*: ἀκριβῶς (accurately, 5×), δωρεάν (freely, 9×), εὐθύς (immediately, 59×), καλῶς (well, 36×), ὁμοθυμαδόν (with one accord, 11×), οὕτως (thus, 208×), παραχρῆμα (immediately, 18×), πῶς (how? 118×), ταχέως (quickly, 10×), ταχύ (quickly, 18×).

- *Adverbs of degree*: λίαν (very, 12×), μάλιστα (especially, 12×), μᾶλλον (more, 81×), σφόδρα (exceedingly, 11×).

## Interpretation

In Romans 11:25–26a, Paul writes, "Lest you be wise in your own sight, I do not want you to be unaware of this mystery, brothers: a partial hardening has come upon Israel, until the fullness of the Gentiles has come in. And in this way [οὕτως] all Israel will be saved."

1. Samuel Lamerson, *English Grammar to Ace New Testament Greek* (Grand Rapids: Zondervan, 2004), 100.

The "mystery" includes a threefold schema: (1) the hardening of part of Israel, (2) the coming in of the fullness of the Gentiles, and (3) the salvation of all Israel. The discussion of the final salvation of Israel often centers on the function of οὕτως. There are at least three possible uses: logical, temporal, or modal (manner).

First, οὕτως could be used to convey a logical connection: "and *in consequence of this process* [11:25b] all Israel will be saved [11:26a]." Because there are only a few instances in Paul where οὕτως has a logical sense,[2] very few scholars affirm this position.

Second, οὕτως could be used to convey a temporal connection: "and *then* all Israel will be saved." For example, this is sense supported by the NEB: "When that has happened, the whole of Israel will be saved." That is, hardening has happened to part of Israel "until" the fullness of the Gentiles has come in; but *then after that*, all Israel will be saved. Such a rendering naturally leads one to suppose a special time of grace for ethnic Israel in the future. The problem with this interpretation is that οὕτως rarely, if ever, has temporal significance.[3]

Third, οὕτως could be used to convey modal connection: "and *in this manner* all Israel will be saved." Although this is by far the majority view, the particular manner signaled by the adverb remains disputed. Most interpreters argue that the "manner" comes from 11:11–24, which verse 25 summarizes. But what precisely is the manner in which all Israel will be saved? Moo maintains that οὕτως is used modally but conveys a temporal idea. He concludes: "God imposes a hardening on most of Israel while Gentiles come into the messianic salvation, with the Gentiles' salvation leading in turn to Israel's jealousy and her own salvation. But this means that *houtōs*, while not having a temporal *meaning*, has a temporal *reference*."[4]

But the question is whether the context argues for a temporal reference. Wright casts doubt on this interpretation: "Paul gives no

---

2. Douglas J. Moo lists Rom. 1:15; 6:11; 1 Cor. 14:25; 1 Thess. 4:17. *The Letter to the Romans*, 2nd ed., NICNT (Grand Rapids: Eerdmans, 2018), 735n796.

3. BDAG does not list a temporal use. For an attempt to justify the temporal meaning, see Pieter W. van der Horst, "'Only Then Will All Israel Be Saved': A Short Note on the Meaning of καὶ οὕτως in Romans 11:26," *JBL* 119 (2000): 521–39. He suggests that Acts 7:8; 20:11; 27:17; and 1 Thess. 4:16–17 support the temporal usage of οὕτως.

4. Moo, *Romans*, 735, emphasis original. See also Thomas R. Schreiner, *Romans*, 2nd ed., BECNT (Grand Rapids: Baker Academic, 2018), 602.

indication that he is talking about a *further* event, but rather gives every indication that this process in 11.25 . . . *is the means by which* God is saving 'all Israel.'"[5] However, if οὕτως is understood to a have a temporal reference, then Paul is claiming that the salvation of "all Israel" takes place after the salvation of every elect Gentile. That is, Israel's salvation takes place after the partial hardening is removed, which will only take place once "the fullness of the Gentiles has come in" (11:25).

The other modal option is to take οὕτως as referring to the process of the salvation of all Israel. That is, Paul is not predicting a future time when the majority of ethnic Jews will embrace Jesus as the Messiah and be saved. Instead, his point is that God will never completely forsake the nation of Israel: there will always be a remnant of believing Jews throughout history until Christ returns. Israel will experience only a *partial* hardening until the end of time (i.e., until the fullness of the Gentiles comes in). They will never be *fully* hardened and rejected from the salvation offered in the Messiah. Thus the sum total of all the elect remnant throughout history represents the salvation of "all Israel." For example, Horne comments, "When Paul states that 'all Israel shall be saved' he means to refer to the full number of elect Jews whom it pleases God to bring into his kingdom throughout the ages until the very day when the full number of Gentiles also shall have been brought in."[6]

Adverbs are important. In the case of Romans 11, the adverb οὕτως indicates the manner in which an action will be accomplished (i.e., the salvation of all Israel). Precisely what the manner refers to is a matter of debate. The point of this chapter is not to argue

5. N. T. Wright, *Paul and the Faithfulness of God*, 2 vols. (Minneapolis: Fortress, 2013), 1241, emphasis original.

6. Charles Horne, "The Meaning of the Phrase 'And Thus All Israel Will Be Saved' (Rom. 11:26)," *JETS* 21 (1978): 334. Likewise William Hendriksen writes: "It is evident . . . that the salvation of 'all Israel' was being progressively realized in Paul's own day and age, and that it will continue to be progressively realized until 'all Israel' shall have been saved. When the full number of elect Gentiles will have been gathered in, then the full number of elect Jews will also have been gathered in. . . . In Elijah's day there was a remnant. In Paul's day there was a remnant. In the years to come there would be a remnant. These remnants of all the ages taken together constitute 'all Israel.'" *Israel in Prophecy* (Grand Rapids: Baker, 1974), 48–49, 50–51.

for a particular view.[7] Rather, it is to demonstrate the significance of an adverb and its relation to our understanding of the Bible and theology.

7. See Michael J. Vlach, Benjamin L. Merkle, Fred G. Zaspel, and James M. Hamilton Jr., *Three Views on Israel and the Church: Perspectives on Romans 9–11*, ed. Jared Compton and Andrew David Naselli (Grand Rapids: Kregel, 2019).

# 28

# CONJUNCTIONS AND PARTICLES

## Philippians 2:12–13

**Introduction**

In Philippians 2:12 Paul exhorts the Philippians believers, "Work out your own salvation with fear and trembling." Although some have suggested that "salvation" (σωτηρία) is used in a sociological sense, referring to the spiritual health and well-being of the community,[1] this interpretation should be rejected since Paul consistently uses σωτηρία to refer to eschatological salvation.[2] If that is the case, does this statement contradict what Paul says elsewhere, that salvation is by grace alone and is not based on works?[3] In other words, how does Paul summon believers "to accomplish their own eschatological deliverance" (Schreiner, *Paul*, 256)?

1. So Gerald F. Hawthorne, *Philippians*, WBC 43 (Waco: Word, 1983), 98–99; Ralph P. Martin, *Philippians*, rev. ed., TNTC (Grand Rapids: Eerdmans, 1987), 115–16.
2. Peter T. O'Brien, *The Epistle to the Philippians*, NIGTC (Grand Rapids: Eerdmans, 1991), 278–81; Thomas R. Schreiner, *Paul: Apostle of God's Glory in Christ* (Downers Grove, IL: InterVarsity, 2001), 256.
3. See Rom. 3:20; 9:11–12; Gal. 2:16; 3:2, 5, 10; Eph. 2:8–9; Titus 3:5.

## Overview

Conjunctions are words that connect or link various literary components together (i.e., words, phrases, clauses, discourse units).[4] Robertson (1177) writes that conjunctions "have a very good name, since they bind together (*con-jungo*) the various parts of speech not otherwise connected, if they need connection, for asyndeton is always possible to the speaker or writer. The point here is to interpret each conjunction as far as possible so that its precise function may be made clear." He indicates that the key is to determine the function of the conjunction since it signals the relationship between discourse units. Young (179) rightly observes that most "sentences in the Greek NT begin with a conjunction. The NT writers follow the classical practice of using conjunctions to indicate semantic relations between sentences and paragraphs." At its basic level, a conjunction indicates whether one unit constitutes a parallel assertion with the other (coordinating conjunction) or whether it is dependent on the other (subordinating conjunction). Various types of conjunctions include the following:

- *Copulative*: καί (and, also); δέ (and); οὐδέ (and not); μηδέ (and not); τέ (and so); οὔτε (and not); μήτε (and not).
- *Disjunctive*: ἤ (or); εἴτε (if, whether).
- *Adversative*: ἀλλά (but); δέ (but); μέν (but); μέντοι (nevertheless); πλήν (but, except); εἰ μή (except); ὅμως (yet); καίτοι (yet).
- *Inferential*: οὖν (therefore, so); ἄρα (then); διό (for this reason); δή (therefore).
- *Explanatory*: γάρ (for).
- *Purpose*: ἵνα (in order that, so that); ὅπως (that).
- *Result*: ὥστε (so that); ὅπως (that).
- *Causal*: ὅτι (that, because); διότι (because); ἐπεί (because, since); ἐπειδή (because).
- *Comparative*: ὡς (as, like); ὥσπερ (just as); καθώς (as, just as); καθάπερ (just as).

---

4. See Steven E. Runge, *Discourse Grammar of the Greek New Testament: A Practical Introduction for Teaching and Exegesis* (Peabody, MA: Hendrickson, 2010).

- *Conditional*: εἰ (if); ἐάν (if); εἴπερ (if indeed).
- *Concessive*: εἰ καί (even if); καὶ εἰ (even if); κἄν (even though); καίπερ (although).
- *Declarative*: ὅτι (that); ἵνα (that).
- *Temporal*: ὅτε (when); ἕως (until); ὅταν (whenever); πρίν (before).
- *Local*: οὗ (where); ὅπου (where); ὅθεν (from where, whence).

A particle is difficult to define and almost seems to be a catchall for words that do not fit into any other part of speech. Particles are usually short (sometimes untranslated) words that can often also be categorized as adverbs, conjunctions, or interjections.

- *Particles of negation*: indicative mood = οὐ, οὐκ, οὐχ, οὐχί; nonindicative moods = μή, μήποτε (never).
- *Particles of connection*: μέν . . . δέ (on the one hand, . . . on the other hand), τέ (and).
- *Particles of intensification*: ἀμήν (amen), γέ (even), ναί (yes!).
- *Particles of interjection*: ἰδού (look!), οὐαί (woe!), ὦ (O!).
- *Particles of the subjunctive mood*: ἄν and ἐάν.

### Interpretation

So, how can it be that Paul urges the Philippian congregation to "work out [their] own salvation with fear and trembling"? The answer to this question lies not in offering a sociological understanding of salvation but in seeing the connection of 2:12 with verse 13. After Paul exhorts the congregation to "work out" (κατεργάζεσθε) their own salvation, he provides the basis for his command: "for [γάρ] it is God who works in you, both to will and to work for his good pleasure." Thus the conjunction γάρ grounds the exhortation in the prior power and ability that God gives. As O'Brien (*Philippians*, 284) comments,

> The Philippians are not left to their own devices *because* (γάρ) God himself is powerfully working in them to achieve his gracious saving purposes in their lives. The conjunction γάρ ("for," "because") shows

that this verse provides the ground for Paul's exhortation in the preceding: *because* God has already begun a good work (of a new creation) in their lives (1:6) and continues it powerfully (ἐνεργῶν), they can be enjoined to work out their salvation with fear and trembling (v. 12).

Biblical scholars sometimes describe the twofold nature of such statements as the relationship between "indicative" and the "imperative." The indicative relates to the reality and results of being united with Christ (the "already"), whereas the imperative flows from the indicative and calls believers to become what they are positionally (the "not yet"). Because believers are united with Christ, they (1) were buried with Christ, have died to sin, and are raised to newness of life (Rom. 6:2–6); (2) have been freed from "the law of sin and death" (Rom. 8:1–2); (3) "are not in the flesh but in the Spirit" (Rom. 8:9); (4) "have been crucified with Christ" and "now live . . . by faith" (Gal. 2:20); (5) "have put on Christ" (Gal. 3:27); (6) are God's children (Gal. 4:6–7); (7) have been made alive, raised, and seated with Christ "in the heavenly places" (Eph. 2:5–6); (8) have died, been buried, and raised with Christ (Col. 2:11–12, 20; 3:1–4); and (9) "have put off the old self" (Col. 3:9).

These indicatives (factual assertions), however, do not remove the need for the imperatives. Thus Paul writes that believers should work out their salvation, and to demonstrate that this should be done with the utmost seriousness, he adds, "with fear and trembling."[5] Similarly, Peter urges his readers, "Give diligence to make your calling and election sure" (2 Pet. 1:10 KJV). Additionally, Paul uses various metaphors to demonstrate the effort needed in pursuing salvation: a pursuit (Rom. 14:19), a pressing on (Phil. 3:12), a fight (1 Cor. 9:26; 1 Tim. 6:12), and a race (1 Cor. 9:24–27).

In Romans 6 Paul asserts that believers have died to sin and that those who have died have been "set free from sin" (v. 7). And yet Paul later commands them, "Therefore do not let sin reign in your mortal body so that you obey its lusts" (v. 12, NASB). The indicative truth (death to sin) does not cancel out the need for the imperative (Don't let sin reign in you). In fact, the indicative is the basis on which the

---

5. This phrase is unique to Paul in the NT (see also 1 Cor. 2:3; 2 Cor. 7:15; Eph. 6:5), though a similar construction appears in Mark 5:33.

imperative *can* be obeyed. Another example is found in Colossians 3 where Paul declares, "For you have died, and your life is hidden with Christ in God" (3:3). A few verses later, he adds, "Put to death therefore what is earthly in you: sexual immorality, impurity, passion, evil desire, and covetousness, which is idolatry" (3:5). Even though they have died with Christ, they still need to put to death the sin in their lives. In essence, then, we are exhorted to become what we already are in Christ. But it is the indicative that "guarantees the imperative will become a reality" (Schreiner, *Paul*, 257).

Thus, in Philippians 2:12 the imperative to work out one's salvation can only be achieved in light of God's prior work in the life of the believer. Ridderbos captures the essence of this discussion: "The word 'for' in the second clause furnishes the ground for the appeal in the first. . . . God does not work and has not worked in his good pleasure because man has worked his salvation with fear and trembling. The contrary is true: because God works and has worked, therefore man must and can work. For God works in him what is necessary for his (human) working."[6]

The link between the imperative and the indicative in Philippians 2:12–13 is the little but highly important word γάρ. It reminds us that as we strive to work out our salvation, we must rely on "the strength that God provides" (1 Pet. 4:11 CSB). Or as Paul put it, "But by the grace of God I am what I am, and his grace toward me was not in vain. On the contrary, I worked harder than any of them, though it was not I, but the grace of God that is with me" (1 Cor. 15:10).

---

6. Herman Ridderbos, *Paul: An Outline of His Theology*, trans. John Richard de Witt (Grand Rapids: Eerdmans, 1975), 255.

# 29

# CONDITIONAL SENTENCES

## Colossians 1:23

**Introduction**

Apparently the false teachers in Colossians were having some success and were wreaking havoc in the church at Colossae. In his letter, Paul rebukes their deficient Christology by elevating Christ to his rightful place. But along the way, Paul warns the Colossian believers that only *if* they persevere in the faith will they be presented holy and blameless before God: "And you, who once were alienated and hostile in mind, doing evil deeds, he has now reconciled in his body of flesh by his death, in order to present you holy and blameless and above reproach before him, <u>if indeed</u> [εἴ γε] you continue in the faith, stable and steadfast, not shifting from the hope of the gospel that you heard" (Col. 1:21–23). In this warning, Paul uses a conditional sentence to state that they will only be presented before God "if [they] continue in the faith." Does this conditional statement by the apostle express doubt or confidence? Is Paul saying, "If you continue in the faith, but it doesn't seem like you will," or is he saying, "If you continue in the faith, and I know that you will"?

## Overview

Conditional clauses are special types of dependent clauses, usually introduced with a conditional particle such as εἰ (if, since) or ἐάν (if).[1] Typically, there are four *classes* of conditional sentences. The protasis signifies the "if" clause, whereas the apodosis signifies the "then" clause, indicating the resulting circumstances if the condition is met. Here is one example for each class:

- *First class*: εἰ + protasis (any tense + ind. mood) and apodosis (any tense/mood): The author assumes the reality of the premise for the sake of argument: "If [εἰ] you are the Son of God, command these stones to become loaves of bread" (Matt. 4:3).
- *Second class*: εἰ + protasis (impf., aor., plupf. + ind. mood) and apodosis (impf., aor., plupf. + ἄν and ind. mood): The premise is contrary to fact for the sake of the argument: "Lord, if [εἰ] you had been here, my brother would not have died [ἂν ἀπέθανεν]" (John 11:21).
- *Third class*: ἐάν + protasis (any tense + subj. mood) and apodosis (any tense/mood): The premise is presented as tentative by the author: "If [ἐάν] we say [εἴπωμεν] we have no sin, we deceive ourselves" (1 John 1:8).
- *Fourth class*: εἰ + protasis (any tense + opt. mood) and apodosis (any tense + opt. mood): The premise is depicted as an unlikely possibility: "But even if [εἰ] you should suffer [πάσχοιτε] for righteousness' sake, you will be blessed" (1 Pet. 3:14).

## Interpretation

According to Moo, Colossians 1:23 contains "a long and complex conditional clause."[2] Most commentators agree that the conditional

---

1. Some adverbial participles (e.g., Luke 9:25) can be translated as conditional clauses.
2. Douglas J. Moo, *The Letters to the Colossians and to Philemon*, PNTC (Grand Rapids: Eerdmans, 2008), 144.

statement is linked to the verb "present" (παραστῆσαι) in the previous verse:[3] Christ, who has reconciled them, will present them holy and blameless before the Father *if* they persevere in the faith. But why does Paul use a conditional statement here? Is he doubting that they will persevere and be saved: "if, though I have my doubts"?[4] Or is he confident that they in fact will persevere and be saved: "if, as I am certain"?[5] By this conditional clause, is Paul affirming that someone might fail to persevere and thus lose their salvation?

The construction that Paul uses is classified as a first-class conditional sentence. There is, however, much confusion as to the meaning and intention of this construction. Basically, this construction indicates that the author affirms something true for the sake of the argument. This does *not* mean, however, that the author necessarily affirms the protasis to be true. Carson calls this assumption a fallacy and states, "In a first-class condition the protasis is assumed true for the sake of the argument, but the thing actually assumed may or may not be true. To put it another way, there is stress on the reality of the assumption, but not on the reality of the content that is assumed."[6] For example, in 1 Corinthians 15:13, Paul declares, "But if [εἰ] there is no resurrection of the dead, then not even Christ has been raised." Here it is obvious that Paul does not actually believe there is no resurrection, since that runs contrary to the very point he is trying to make. Instead, he is making an argument by appealing to something that is not true.

For at least two reasons, many grammarians do not think it is wise to translate first-class conditional sentences with "since."[7]

3. So Murray J. Harris, *Colossians and Philemon*, EGGNT (Nashville: B&H, 2010), 54; Moo, *Colossians and Philemon*, 144; David W. Pao, *Colossians and Philemon*, ZECNT (Grand Rapids: Zondervan, 2012), 109. It is possible, but not as likely, that the conditional clause is linked to the earlier verb "he has reconciled" (ἀποκατήλλαξεν) in Col. 1:22.
4. See Gal. 3:4, "Did you suffer so many things in vain—if indeed [εἴ γε] it was in vain?"
5. See 2 Cor. 5:3, "if indeed [εἴ γε], having been clothed, we shall not be found naked" (NKJV); Eph. 3:2, "if indeed [εἴ γε] you have heard of the stewardship of God's grace which was given to me for you" (NASB); and Eph. 4:21, "if indeed [εἴ γε] you have heard Him and have been taught in Him, just as truth is in Jesus" (NASB).
6. D. A. Carson, *Exegetical Fallacies*, 2nd ed. (Grand Rapids: Baker, 1996), 77.
7. So M&E 235–37; Porter, *Idioms*, 256–57; Wallace 692–93.

First, as we have illustrated above, many first-class conditions are not true in reality. In fact, by one count, only 37 percent are deemed true based on context (and could be translated as "since"), and at least 12 percent (36 instances) are deemed to be false (and could *not* be translated as "since").[8] Second, by using "since" instead of "if" (even when the author is confident of the outcome), the rhetorical effect is lost. That is, by using a conditional statement, the author is challenging the readers to genuinely consider the condition presented. If Paul merely wanted to communicate certainty, he could have used ἐπεί or ἐπειδή (since). Even though Moo thinks that Paul does have confidence in the faith of his readers, he adds, "Nevertheless, the condition is a real one, and it is very important not to rob the words of their intended rhetorical function" (*Colossians and Philemon*, 144). Therefore, Paul's warning needs to be taken with "great seriousness" (144). Thus the statement is a call and motivation for the Colossian Christians to be faithful to the apostolic gospel. Schreiner and Caneday assert that the "if indeed" does not signify confidence but "lays great stress on the condition as absolutely essential for the attainment of being presented holy in God's sight."[9] Hence Paul's admonition means that Christ "will present you holy before him, . . . assuming for the sake of argument (and that is precisely what I am doing) that you persevere in your faith" (*Race Set before Us*, 192).

Ultimately Paul is affirming the need for believers to persevere in their faith in order to have hope on the final day. Yes, believers are saved by grace through faith. And yet believers also need to continue in their belief. If believers do not persevere, they will not be saved. A believer's perseverance in the faith is *conditioned* on, but not *the basis for*, Christ's presentation of the believer to God. Thus Paul "wants to confront the Colossians with the reality that their eventual salvation depends on their remaining faithful to Christ and to the true gospel.

8. James L. Boyer, "First-Class Conditions: What Do They Mean?," *GTJ* 2, no. 1 (1981): 75–114. The remaining 51 percent are undetermined as to whether they are true or false.
9. Thomas R. Schreiner and Ardel B. Caneday, *The Race Set before Us: A Biblical Theology of Perseverance and Assurance* (Downers Grove, IL: InterVarsity, 2001), 192.

Only by continuing in their faith can they hope to find a favorable verdict from God on the day of judgment."[10]

Paul's use of a conditional statement does not mean that he affirms that believers can lose their salvation. The warning is real: those who do not continue in their faith will be judged. The warning, then, becomes "one of the means which the apostle uses to insure that his readers . . . do not fall into a state of false security" and "to stir them up."[11] The condition is real. The warning is real. And yet the grace of God that sustains believers, enabling them to persevere in the faith, is also real.

---

10. Moo, *Colossians and Philemon*, 144. He continues, "God does, indeed, by his grace and through his Spirit, work to preserve his people so that they will be vindicated in the judgment; but, at the same time, God's people are responsible to persevere in their faith if they expect to see that vindication" (144).
11. Peter T. O'Brien, *Colossians, Philemon*, WBC 44 (Waco: Word, 1982), 69.

# 30

# FIGURES OF SPEECH

## Matthew 5:13

### Introduction

In the Sermon on the Mount, Jesus tells his disciples, "You are the salt of the earth, but if salt has lost its taste, how shall its saltiness be restored? It is no longer good for anything except to be thrown out and trampled under people's feet" (Matt. 5:13). In the first part of this verse, Jesus uses a metaphor: "You are the salt of the earth." Although it might seem that the point of comparison is obvious, there are many possible uses of salt in the ancient world. In fact, Davies and Allison list eleven possible views.[1] The two most common views are of (1) salt as a flavor enhancer (seasoning) and (2) salt as a preservative. The point could be that just as salt makes food taste better, so the presence of Christians makes the world a better place in which to live. Or the focus could be that just as salt preserves food, so the presence of Christians should have a preserving effect on the world, protecting it from moral decline. What precisely is the point of comparison?

1. W. D. Davies and Dale C. Allison, *A Critical and Exegetical Commentary on the Gospel according to Matthew*, ICC, 3 vols. (Edinburgh: T&T Clark, 1988), 1:472–73.

## Overview

Young (235) defines a figure of speech as "an expression that uses words in an unusual or nonliteral sense for the purpose of emphasis, clarity, or freshness of thought." It is crucial for the reader of the Bible to understand these literary features so as to correctly interpret the intention of the author. The following list represents various types of figurative language in the NT:[2]

### Statements of Comparison

- *Simile* (an explicit comparison employing "like" or "as"): "The devil prowls around like a roaring lion" (1 Pet. 5:8).
- *Metaphor* (an implied comparison): "The tongue is a fire" (James 3:6).

### Statements of Fullness

- *Pleonasm* (a redundant statement): "He answered and said" (Matt. 4:4 NASB).
- *Paronomasia* (words similar in sound and placed together for emphasis): "And God is able to make all [πᾶσαν] grace abound to you, so that having all [πᾶσαν] sufficiency in all things [παντί] at all times [πάντοτε], you may abound in every [πᾶν] good work" (2 Cor. 9:8).
- *Epizeuxis* (a key word repeated for emphasis): "Holy, holy, holy, is the Lord God Almighty" (Rev. 4:8).

2. These examples generally follow Grant R. Osborne, *The Hermeneutical Spiral: A Comprehensive Introduction to Biblical Interpretation*, rev. and exp. (Downers Grove, IL: InterVarsity, 2006), 124–29. See also Walter C. Kaiser and Moisés Silva, *An Introduction to Biblical Hermeneutics: The Search for Meaning* (Grand Rapids: Zondervan, 1994), 92–98; William W. Klein, Craig L. Blomberg, and Robert L. Hubbard Jr., *Introduction to Biblical Interpretation*, 3rd ed. (Grand Rapids: Zondervan, 2017), 361–413; Andreas J. Köstenberger and Richard D. Patterson, *Invitation to Biblical Interpretation: Exploring the Hermeneutical Triad of History, Literature, and Theology* (Grand Rapids: Kregel, 2011), 663–83; A. Berkeley Mickelsen, *Interpreting the Bible* (Grand Rapids: Eerdmans, 1963), 178–98; Andrew David Naselli, *How to Understand and Apply the New Testament: Twelve Steps from Exegesis to Theology* (Phillipsburg, NJ: P&R, 2017), 17–19.

- *Hendiadys* (two terms used to express the same idea): "while we wait for <u>the blessed hope</u> and <u>appearing of the glory of our great God and Savior,</u> Jesus Christ" (Titus 2:13 HCSB).

## Incomplete Statements

- *Ellipsis* (a grammatically incomplete expression): "Do we not have the right to eat and [<u>the right to</u>] drink" (1 Cor. 9:4).
- *Zeugma* ("a special type of ellipsis requiring a different verb to be supplied," BDF §479.2, p. 253): "who forbid marriage <u>and advocate</u> abstaining from foods which God has created" (1 Tim. 4:3 NASB).

## Statements of Contrast or Understatements

- *Irony* (intending to communicate the opposite of what is stated): "Already you have all you want! Already you have become rich! Without us you have become kings! And would that you did reign, so that we might share the rule with you!" (1 Cor. 4:8).
- *Litotes* (an assertion is made by negating its opposite): "Paul and Barnabas had <u>no small dissension and debate</u>" = a great dissension and debate (Acts 15:2).
- *Euphemism* (a nicer way to communicate a harsher term): "and for all who are far off" = Gentiles (Acts 2:39).

## Statements of Exaggeration

- *Overstatement* (an exaggerated statement that is possible to accomplish, though not intended to be): "If your right eye causes you to sin, tear it out and throw it away" (Matt. 5:29).
- *Hyperbole* (an exaggerated statement that is impossible to accomplish): "It is easier for a camel to go through the eye of a needle than for a rich person to enter the kingdom of God" (Matt. 19:24).

### Statements of Association or Relation

- *Metonymy* (one noun substituted for another that is closely associated with it): "If they do not listen to <u>Moses</u> [= the Pentateuch] and the Prophets" (Luke 16:31 NASB).
- *Synecdoche* (a part is substituted for the whole or the whole for the part): "Give us this day our <u>daily bread</u>" (Matt. 6:11).

### Statements Stressing a Personal Dimension

- *Personification* (human characteristics given to an inanimate object or concept): "Therefore do not be anxious about tomorrow, for tomorrow will be anxious for itself" (Matt. 6:34).
- *Anthropomorphism* (human characteristics attributed to God): "Jesus . . . is seated at the <u>right hand</u> of the throne of God" (Heb. 12:2).

## Interpretation

A metaphor can have three parts: (1) the *topic* that is being discussed, (2) the *image* with which the topic is compared, and (3) the *point of similarity* or comparison (see Young 236). Some metaphors are complete (having all three components); others can be classified as incomplete (missing one or two of the components). The metaphor in Matthew 5:13, "You are the salt of the world" (ISV), contains the topic (you) and the image (salt), but the point of similarity is lacking. Thus, because it is not obvious (at least to us), the reader has to decide the point of comparison that Jesus intended. Is the emphasis on the flavor-enhancing quality of salt or the preserving quality of salt?

Such a question is not necessarily easy to answer. Keener argues that the focus is on salt as flavor enhancer since that was often what was in view in contemporary literature when discussing the function of salt.[3] Others argue that the preserving function of salt is the point of similarity. For example, Carson suggests, "The point is that, if

3. Craig S. Keener, *The Gospel of Matthew: A Socio-Rhetorical Commentary* (Grand Rapids: Eerdmans, 2009), 173.

Jesus' disciples are to act as a preservative in the world by conforming to kingdom norms, if they are 'called to be a moral disinfectant in a world where moral standards are low, constantly changing, or nonexistent . . . they can discharge this function only if they themselves retain their virtue.'"[4] Likewise Blomberg maintains that salt's "use as a preservative in food was probably its most basic function."[5] Thus "Christians must permeate society as agents of redemption" in order "to arrest corruption and prevent moral decay in their world."[6]

Most commentators, however, are convinced that both aspects of comparison are in view.[7] Osborne explains, "Due to the breadth of the metaphor, it is impossible to single out any one, and it is best to allow multiple aspects."[8] This interpretation seems possible since the same salt that would be used to preserve meat would also add flavor to that meat. Therefore the metaphor "means simply to make an impact on the world"—an impact made by penetrating the world with the presence of the gospel witness in both word and deed (Osborne, *Matthew*, 175).

4. D. A. Carson, "Matthew," in *The Expositor's Bible Commentary*, ed. Tremper Longman III and David E. Garland, rev. ed. (Grand Rapids: Zondervan, 2010), 9:169, quoting R. V. G. Tasker, *The Gospel according to St. Matthew: An Introduction and Commentary*, TNTC (Grand Rapids: Eerdmans, 1961).

5. Craig L. Blomberg, *Matthew*, NAC 22 (Nashville: Broadman & Holman, 1992), 102.

6. Blomberg, *Matthew*, 102. He further argues, "It is not likely that many ancient Jews considered salt primarily as enhancing taste" (102).

7. R. T. France, *The Gospel of Matthew*, NICNT (Grand Rapids: Eerdmans, 2007), 174; Leon Morris, *The Gospel according to Matthew*, PNTC (Grand Rapids: Eerdmans, 1992), 104; Grant R. Osborne, *Matthew*, ZECNT (Grand Rapids: Zondervan, 2010), 175; David L. Turner, *Matthew*, BECNT (Grand Rapids: Baker Academic, 2008), 154–55.

8. Osborne, *Matthew*, 175. One has to be careful, however, of the exegetical fallacy termed "illegitimate totality transfer" (see chap. 33 below).

# 31

# CONTEXT

## Philippians 4:13

### Introduction

There is no doubt that Philippians 4:13 is one of the most well-known and quoted verses. In fact, after John 3:16, Philippians 4:13 is often the most-searched Bible verse on the internet. We have all seen or heard of athletes who claim this verse before and during a game, and several famous athletes have the reference written on parts of their body or featured on their clothing. It contains ten words in English and only six words in Greek: "I can do all things through him who strengthens me" (πάντα ἰσχύω ἐν τῷ ἐνδυναμοῦντί με). This seems to be an incredible verse that includes an all-encompassing promise. But does the verse really mean that when Christians are empowered by Christ, nothing is beyond their capabilities? That when they trust in Christ and believe something in their heart, they will be able to do whatever they set their mind to accomplish? In other words, what does Paul mean when he says he can do "all things" through Christ, who gives him strength?

### Overview

Context is king. This means that when studying a passage of Scripture, the context of a passage is what determines its meaning. Robert

Stein defines literary context as "the communicative intent of the author found in the words, sentences, paragraphs, and chapters surrounding a passage."[1] This includes not only the immediately surrounding material but also the entire book (and ultimately the entire canon).[2] Words derive their meaning from the literary context. Jeannine Brown comments, "The method of reading select passages here and there, which is rather common in the Christian tradition, can lead to misreading if the literary context is ignored."[3] Kaiser and Silva illustrate the absurdity of attempting to understand a passage in a letter without knowledge of the whole letter: "What would one think of a man who receives a five-page letter from his fiancée on Monday and decides to read only the third page on that day, the last page on Thursday, the first page two weeks later, and so on? We are all aware of the fact that reading a letter in such piece-meal fashion would likely create nothing but confusion."[4] Consequently, Kaiser and Silva (*Biblical Hermeneutics*, 64) insist that reading a passage in context is "the fundamental principle" that "undergirds" all other principles. Duvall and Hays maintain that "the most important principle of biblical interpretation is that *context determines meaning.*"[5] Mickelsen (*Interpreting the Bible*, 99) warns, "Neglect of context is a common cause of erroneous interpretation and irrelevant application."

## Interpretation

Those who are serious about studying the Bible know that a passage can be rightly understood only in its context. Discerning the

1. Robert H. Stein, *A Basic Guide to Interpreting the Bible: Playing by the Rules*, 2nd ed. (Grand Rapids: Baker Academic, 2011), 53.

2. Stein (*Basic Guide*, 53) suggests, "The immediate literary context surrounding a passage is the most valuable."

3. Jeannine K. Brown, *Scripture as Communication: Introducing Biblical Hermeneutics* (Grand Rapids: Baker Academic, 2007), 214.

4. Walter C. Kaiser and Moisés Silva, *An Introduction to Biblical Hermeneutics: The Search for Meaning* (Grand Rapids: Zondervan, 1994), 123. A. Berkeley Mickelsen similarly asserts that the original readers of the NT letters "did not plunge into the middle of the letter and seize out a few consecutive sentences. They read carefully the whole document." *Interpreting the Bible* (Grand Rapids: Eerdmans, 1963), 104.

5. J. Scott Duvall and J. Daniel Hays, *Grasping God's Word: A Hands-On Approach to Reading, Interpreting, and Applying the Bible*, 2nd ed. (Grand Rapids: Zondervan, 2005), 119.

appropriate meaning of a word, phrase, sentence, or verse is only possible when the context is known. When something is taken out of context, it can be used in a manner in which it was never intended. For example, I have often thought that Revelation 11:10 would make a great verse for a Christmas card: "Those who dwell on the earth will rejoice over them and make merry and exchange presents." The reason that this verse should *never* be used in connection with Christmas relates to its context. The verse is not talking about Christians who are rejoicing at the birth of their Savior but about the enemies of God who killed his two prophets and celebrated in response to their (apparent) victory over God's people. To apply that text to Christmas would be akin to ripping a child from the arms of its mother.

So what is the context of Philippians 4:13? Usually a question related to the context of the passage needs to be asked in two parts: (1) What is the broad context? and (2) What is the immediate context? The broad context of Philippians 4:13 is the entire Epistle of Philippians. Paul established the church in Philippi on his second missionary journey (Acts 16:6–15) and had visited the church at least three times before writing his letter to them (Acts 16; 20:1–2, 6). The church was very generous in their giving (Phil. 4:15–18; 2 Cor. 8:1–4). When the apostle Paul wrote this letter, he was under house arrest (Phil. 1:7, 13, 17) in Rome (1:13; 4:22) from AD 60 to 62, about thirty years after his conversion.

Paul also recognizes that death may be the outcome of his imprisonment. He states, "[I hope that] Christ will be honored in my body, whether by life or by death. For to me to live is Christ, and to die is gain" (1:20–21). He later mentions being "poured out as a drink offering" (2:17). But although Paul realizes that his situation is serious, he also anticipates the possibility of soon being released (1:19, 25–26; 2:23–24).

Understanding the immediate context of Philippians 4:13 is also vital to correctly understanding this verse. What precisely does Paul mean by "all things"? Certainly this cannot mean that Paul thought he could do *anything* through Christ's power. Indeed, the preceding verses clarify Paul's statement. In verses 11–12 he declares, "Not that I am speaking of being in need, for I have learned in whatever situation I am to be content. I know how to be brought low, and I know how to abound. In any [παντί] and every [πᾶσιν] circumstance, I have learned the secret of facing plenty and hunger, abundance and need." Paul states that he learned to live contently in any circumstance or situation. He knew how to be content with much ("abound," "plenty," "abundance") and with little ("brought low," "hunger," "need"). The key phrase is found in verse 12, where Paul states "in any [παντί] and every [πᾶσιν] circumstance." The Greek terms παντί and πᾶσιν are derivatives from πᾶς, which is the same Greek word that is behind the translation of "all things" (πάντα). The "all things" of verse 13, then, refers back to "any and every circumstance" in verse 12. Thus, when Paul writes "all things," he is specifically referring to all those situations or circumstances that he faces, some of them good and some of them extremely difficult. In light of this context, Hawthorne is correct in declaring, "Those translations which give the impression that Paul meant he could do anything and that nothing was beyond his powers . . . are misleading to the point of being false. . . . Πάντα as used here can only refer to 'all those situations,' both good and bad, that have just been described."[6] Because of his union with Christ, Paul was receiving sufficient strength to persevere. The secret of Paul's contentment, regardless of his situation, was to rest in the strength that Christ provides. In other words, his secret was that *he* didn't do all these things; *Christ* did them through him.

Another cause for misunderstanding this verse is the translation of ἰσχύω as "I can do." This verb does not mean "do" but to "be strong, powerful, able, prevail over."[7] In fact, the term is used twenty-seven other times in the NT and never translated as "do." To help demonstrate the meaning of this verb, here are three examples (trans. author):

- A demon-possessed man "prevailed over" (ἴσχυσεν) the seven sons of Sceva (Acts 19:16).

6. Gerald F. Hawthorne, *Philippians*, WBC 43 (Waco: Word, 1983), 200–201. The NIV 2011 helped correct this misunderstanding when it changed from "I can do everything through him who gives me strength" (NIV 1984) to "I can do all this through him who gives me strength" (NIV 2011). The phrase "all this" drives the reader back to the preceding verses to find the answer. The CEB is perhaps even better: "I can endure all these things through the power of the one who gives me strength."
7. BDAG 484, "have power," "be competent," "be able."

- "So the word of the Lord flourished and prevailed [ἴσχυεν]" (Acts 19:20).
- The dragon could not "prevail over" (ἴσχυσεν) Michael and his angels (Rev. 12:8).

From these (and other) examples, it is clear that Paul is not talking about what we can *do* but about prevailing or having the victory over something. That is, he is not claiming that he can *do* all things through Christ, but rather that he can *prevail over* (win, have the victory over) any circumstance he faces by relying on Christ and his strength. The verse can be accurately paraphrased: "I can have the victory (prevail) over any circumstance through my union with Christ, who continually strengthens me."

Philippians 4:13 is not primarily about the great accomplishments that we attempt. It's not about winning a sporting event or about achieving the victory of that next milestone in our lives. The meaning of this verse is not so much about what we do as about what is done (or what happens) to us. Brown comments, "By pulling Philippians 4:13 out of its literary context, we miss the invitation to learn contentment by relying on the Lord's strength—an invitation that is thoroughly countercultural" (*Scripture as Communication*, 216).

# 32

# WORD STUDIES

## Ephesians 1:10

### Introduction

In the opening chapter of Ephesians, Paul offers at least four reasons why Christians should praise ("bless") God: because he (1) chose us (1:3–6), (2) redeems us (1:7–10), (3) provides an inheritance for us (1:11–12), and (4) seals us with his Holy Spirit (1:13–14). The second section, which highlights our redemption, states, "In him we have redemption through his blood, the forgiveness of our trespasses, according to the riches of his grace, which he lavished upon us, in all wisdom and insight making known to us the mystery of his will, according to his purpose, which he set forth in Christ as a plan for the fullness of time, to unite all things in him, things in heaven and things on earth" (Eph. 1:7–10). Verse 10, which many commentators maintain is the high point of the eulogy,[1] indicates that God's plan is for Christ to unite all things. In this context Paul declares that God set forth Christ as an οἰκονομίαν "for the fullness of time." But what exactly does Paul mean by οἰκονομία in this passage?

---

1. See, e.g., Ernest Best, *Ephesians*, ICC (London: T&T Clark, 1998), 139.

## Overview

Oftentimes when we study a passage of Scripture, we are confronted with terms or phrases that are not altogether clear to us. When that is the case, it is often beneficial to take the time to study the word in more detail—especially when a word is (1) theologically important, (2) repeated, (3) unclear or difficult, or (4) has a figurative meaning. Here are seven helpful steps to properly study a word:[2]

1. Consider the immediate and broader literary context.
2. Compare English Bible translations.
3. Consider the same biblical author's other uses of the word.
4. List the possible definitions of the word according to standard lexicons.
5. Identify other words in the same semantic domain.
6. Consider uses of the word throughout the NT and the LXX.
7. State your discoveries clearly and succinctly.

## Interpretation

1. *Consider the immediate and broader literary context.* Ephesians 1:10 (and thus the word οἰκονομία) is found in the first half of the body of the letter (1:3–3:21) and is located amid an extended praise to God for his blessings that believers receive from their union with Christ (1:3–14). This blessing or eulogy precedes the thanksgiving section that is typical of most of Paul's epistles. In Greek, this paragraph consists of one long sentence (202 words).

2. I will be following the steps as presented in KMP 484–89. See also J. Scott Duvall and J. Daniel Hays, *Grasping God's Word: A Hands-On Approach to Reading, Interpreting, and Applying the Bible*, 2nd ed. (Grand Rapids: Zondervan, 2005), 135–52; William W. Klein, Craig L. Blomberg, and Robert L. Hubbard Jr., *Introduction to Biblical Interpretation*, 3rd ed. (Grand Rapids: Zondervan, 2017), 324–44; Andrew David Naselli, *How to Understand and Apply the New Testament: Twelve Steps from Exegesis to Theology* (Phillipsburg, NJ: P&R, 2017), 206–29; Grant R. Osborne, *The Hermeneutical Spiral: A Comprehensive Introduction to Biblical Interpretation*, rev. and exp. (Downers Grove, IL: InterVarsity, 2006), 93–112; Henry A. Virkler and Karelynne Gerber Ayayo, *Hermeneutics: Principles and Processes of Biblical Interpretation*, 2nd ed. (Grand Rapids: Baker Academic, 2007), 97–117.

2. *Compare English Bible translations.* Because οἰκονομία is the object of a preposition εἰς, I will provide the translation of the entire prepositional phrase.

| English Bible Versions | Rendering of **οἰκονομία** |
|---|---|
| ESV (also CSB, RSV, NRSV) | "as a plan" |
| NLT | "And this is the plan" |
| CEB | "This is what God planned" |
| HCSB | "for the administration" |
| NASB | "with a view to an administration" |
| NET | "toward the administration" |
| NKJV (also KJV) | "that in the dispensation" |
| NIV | "to be put into effect when" |
| NJB | "for him to act upon" |

You can see that there is a wide range of translations, with three terms being the most common: "plan" (CSB, ESV, NLT, NRSV, RSV; cf. CEB), "administration" (HCSB, NASB, NET), and "dispensation" (KJV, NKJV). Some of the more dynamic translations change the noun to a verbal idea: "planned" (CEB), "to be put into effect" (NIV), and "to act upon" (NJB).

3. *Consider the same biblical author's other uses of the word.* The term οἰκονομία occurs nine times in the NT, six of them in Paul's writings.

- "For if I do this of my own will, I have a reward, but if not of my own will, I am still entrusted with a <u>stewardship</u> [οἰκονομίαν]" (1 Cor. 9:17).
- "assuming that you have heard of <u>the stewardship</u> [τὴν οἰκονομίαν] of God's grace that was given to me for you" (Eph. 3:2).
- "and to bring to light for everyone what is <u>the plan</u> [ἡ οἰκονομία] of the mystery hidden for ages in God, who created all things" (Eph. 3:9).
- "of which I became a minister according to <u>the stewardship</u> [τὴν οἰκονομίαν] from God that was given to me for you, to make the word of God fully known" (Col. 1:25).

- "nor to devote themselves to myths and endless genealogies, which promote speculations rather than the <u>stewardship</u> [οἰκονομίαν] from God that is by faith" (1 Tim. 1:4).

In three of these texts, Paul is describing the "stewardship" that was given to him by God (1 Cor. 9:17; Eph. 3:2; Col. 1:25). In addition 1 Timothy 1:4 refers to a "stewardship" that is given by God.[3] Consequently, Ephesians 3:9 is the closest usage to what we find in 1:10 since both texts refer to God's "plan." Perhaps this is why the ESV translated the other uses as "stewardship" but Ephesians 1:10 and 3:9 as "plan."

4. *List the possible definitions of the word according to standard lexicons.* Notice the various meanings of οἰκονομία in Scripture:

- BDAG 697–98: (1) "responsibility of management, management of a household" (Luke 16:2–4; 1 Cor. 9:17; Eph. 3:2; Col. 1:25); (2) "arrangement, order, plan," such as "God's unique private plan, plan of salvation" (Eph. 1:10; 3:9); (3) "program of instruction" (1 Tim. 1:4).
- *NIDNTTE* 3:465–69: "household management," "office," "task," "plan." Silva notes that Paul's use of οἰκονομία "is the most distinctive" in relating to "God's plan of salvation."
- L&N: (1) task: "a task involving management and organization" (42.25); (2) plan: "a plan which involves a set of arrangements (referring in the NT to God's plan for bringing salvation to mankind within the course of history)" (30.68); (3) manage a household: "to run a household, to be in charge of household" (46.1).

5. *Identify other words in the same semantic domain.* The following entries are found in L&N under the same semantic domain as

3. The ESV interprets οἰκονομίαν θεοῦ as "stewardship from God," a genitive of source. It could also be interpreted as a possessive genitive ("God's plan") or subjective genitive ("God plans [something]"), in which case its use would be similar to Eph. 1:10 (so L&N 30.68).

οἰκονομία and with the meaning of "to intend, to purpose, to plan" (30.56–30.74).[4]

- βούλημα, βουλή: "that which has been purposed and planned—'plan, intention, purpose'"
- θέλημα: "that which is purposed, intended, or willed—'will, intent, purpose, plan'"
- πρόθεσις: "that which is planned or purposed in advance—'plan, proposal, purpose'"
- ἔννοια, ἐπίνοια: "that which is intended or purposed as the result of thinking—'intention, purpose'"
- γνώμη: "that which is purposed or intended, with the implication of judgment or resolve—'purpose, intention'"
- ἐπιβουλή: "a plan for treacherous activity against someone—'plot, plan, scheme'"
- συστροφή: "a plan devised by a number of persons who agree to act against someone or some institution—'plot, scheme, conspiracy'"
- συνωμοσία: "a plan for taking secret action against someone or some institution, with the implication of an oath binding the conspirators—'conspiracy, plot'"

6. *Consider uses of the word throughout the NT and LXX.* The other three uses of οἰκονομία occur within one passage in the parable of the dishonest manager. In each instance, the reference is to the management of a household—a usage that differs from Ephesians 1:10.

And he called him and said to him, "What is this that I hear about you? Turn in the account of your <u>management</u> [οἰκονομίας], for you can no longer be manager." And the manager said to himself, "What shall I do, since my master is taking the <u>management</u> [οἰκονομίαν] away from me? I am not strong enough to dig, and I am ashamed to beg. I have decided what to do, so that when I am removed from <u>management</u> [οἰκονομίας], people may receive me into their houses." (Luke 16:2–4)

4. I have limited the entries to noun forms only.

Similarly, in the Septuagint, the term appears only twice and in the same context. In Isaiah 22, the Lord is punishing those who abused their office. Consequently, the Lord will take away their office and give it to his chosen servant. Again, this usage differs from what is found in Ephesians 1:10. "And you will be removed from your office [οἰκονομίας] and from your position. . . . And [I] will clothe him with your robe and give him your crown, and I will give your power and office [οἰκονομίαν] into his hands, and he shall be as a father to those who dwell in Jerusalem and to those who dwell in Judah" (Isa. 22:19, 21 NETS altered).

7. *State your discoveries clearly and succinctly.* The term οἰκονομία has three basic uses: (1) the act of administering, (2) that which is administered (i.e., a plan), and (3) the office of an administrator (stewardship). When it is used in the Septuagint (Isa. 22) and elsewhere in the NT (Luke 16), it clearly refers to an office. Three times Paul uses the term to refer to his unique apostolic office given to him by God (1 Cor. 9:17; Eph. 3:2; Col. 1:25). Twice in Paul it refers to God's active working out of his sovereign purpose. In Ephesians 1:10, as the object of the preposition εἰς, the translation "administration" is probably best since it conveys a more active role as opposed to the more passive sense of "plan," where κατά might be expected.[5] It refers to "God's activity of administration."[6] Those English versions that take more liberty and render εἰς οἰκονομίαν with a verbal idea have captured the sense of the phrase (CEB, NIV, NJB).[7] The translation "dispensation" should probably not be used, since it is based on the Latin and could confuse readers with notions of modern "dispensationalism." Thus the usage of οἰκονομία refers to "God's work of administering the plan that he decided on according to his good pleasure" (Thielman, *Ephesians*, 64).

---

5. Best, *Ephesians*, 139; William J. Larkin, *Ephesians: A Handbook on the Greek Text*, Baylor Handbook on the Greek New Testament (Waco: Baylor University Press, 2009), 12; Andrew T. Lincoln, *Ephesians*, WBC 42 (Dallas: Word, 1990), 32; Frank Thielman, *Ephesians*, BECNT (Grand Rapids: Baker Academic, 2010), 64.

6. Harold W. Hoehner, *Ephesians: An Exegetical Commentary* (Grand Rapids: Baker Academic, 2002), 218.

7. Hoehner (*Ephesians*, 218) notes, "The translation of the NEB and NIV, 'to be put into effect,' makes good sense."

# 33

# EXEGETICAL FALLACIES

## John 21:15–17

**Introduction**

Many of us have heard preachers wax eloquently regarding the original meaning of some Greek word or phrase. Although such preachers often make confident assertions about the Greek text, their insights are sometimes misinformed, causing biblical scholars to cringe. While we readily acknowledge that knowing Biblical Greek greatly improves our ability to correctly interpret the Bible, having a full-orbed understanding of the language is crucial to help avoid making exegetical errors. One frequently disputed text is Jesus's interaction with Simon Peter in John 21:15–17 (excerpted from HCSB):

> Jesus: "<u>Do you love</u> [ἀγαπᾷς] Me more than these?"
> Peter: "Yes, Lord, You know that <u>I love</u> [φιλῶ] You."
> Jesus: "<u>Do you love</u> [ἀγαπᾷς] Me?"
> Peter: "Yes, Lord, You know that <u>I love</u> [φιλῶ] You."
> Jesus: "<u>Do you love</u> [φιλεῖς] Me?"

Peter: "Lord, You know everything! You know that I love [φιλῶ] You."

Is there significance to the switch in verbs from ἀγαπάω to φιλέω, or is it a mere stylistic variation?

## Overview

Merriam-Webster's dictionary defines *fallacy* as "a wrong belief" or "a false or mistaken idea." An exegetical fallacy is when a mistaken idea is applied to the interpretation and explanation of the Bible. The following four exegetical fallacies are commonly committed.

1. *Etymological fallacy.* This fallacy involves the belief that the original meaning of a word must be related to the later usage of the word. But the root meaning of a word may or may not help us understand what a word actually meant at the time it was used. Because words often change meaning over time, the original meaning of a word may not be significant for interpreting a later usage of a word. For example, "nice" in the eighteenth century meant "precise" and comes from a Latin word (*nescius*) meaning "ignorant." A biblical example that is commonly referred to is the term ὑπηρέτης (servant, assistant), which comes from the two words ὑπό (under) plus ἐρέτης (rower). Thus the assumption is that ὑπηρέτης means "under rower" or "one who is part of a crew rowing a boat." But it is doubtful that Paul was thinking of the root meaning (a rowing metaphor) when he wrote 1 Corinthians 4:1, "This is how one should regard us, as servants [ὑπηρέτας] of Christ and stewards of the mysteries of God."

2. *Subsequent meaning fallacy (semantic anachronism).* This fallacy involves reading a later meaning back into an earlier usage of a term. Our goal is to discover what a biblical word meant when it was used, not how it later influenced the creation or meanings of other words. For example, mentioning that the Greek term δύναμις (power) is related to the English word

*dynamite* is irrelevant and perhaps even misleading for understanding the Greek term. It is also unhelpful to claim that "God
loves a *hilarious* giver" (2 Cor. 9:7) simply because the Greek
term ἱλαρός (cheerful) has led to the English word "hilarious."

3. *Illegitimate totality transfer.* This fallacy involves attributing
all (or many) possible meanings of a word to the word's meaning in a specific context. Many words typically have a range of
meanings, but in a given context, only one of those meanings
is relevant.[1] Thus the meaning of a word in a specific context
may not be as wide as the range of possible meanings of that
word. This is the (unintentional) error of the Amplified Bible,
which often includes several possible meanings of various terms.
For example, in the Beatitudes the term "blessed" (μακάριος) is
given the additional meanings of (1) "spiritually prosperous,"
(2) "happy," (3) "to be envied" (Matt. 5:3). In the next eight
verses (Matt. 5:4–11), the Amplified Bible lists fourteen other
amplified meanings of the same Greek term.

4. *Improper relationship between synonyms.* This fallacy is based
on the assumption that every variation in wording is theologically motivated and fails to allow for mere stylistic variation.[2]

## Interpretation

It is frequently taught that ἀγαπάω refers to a divine or sacrificial love
and φιλέω refers to brotherly love. Consequently, in John 21:15–17
the first two times Jesus (or, more accurately, John) uses ἀγαπάω, it
denotes a divine type of love, while Peter can only affirm a brotherly
(or lower) type of love (φιλέω). But the third time Jesus lowers the

1. There are, of course, exceptions to this "rule," especially in the Gospel of John.
2. For an overview of exegetical fallacies, see D. A. Carson, *Exegetical Fallacies*,
2nd ed. (Grand Rapids: Baker, 1996); Andreas J. Köstenberger and Richard D. Patterson, *Invitation to Biblical Interpretation: Exploring the Hermeneutical Triad of
History, Literature, and Theology* (Grand Rapids: Kregel, 2011), 630–50; Andrew
David Naselli, *How to Understand and Apply the New Testament: Twelve Steps from
Exegesis to Theology* (Phillipsburg, NJ: P&R, 2017), 212–16; Grant R. Osborne, *The
Hermeneutical Spiral: A Comprehensive Introduction to Biblical Interpretation*, rev.
and exp. (Downers Grove, IL: InterVarsity, 2006), 82–93.

bar and asks Peter if he loves him with a brotherly love. There are two main reasons why this interpretation of the passage is probably not correct.

First, although John uses two different terms, their range of meanings can overlap. Ἀγαπάω is almost always used in a positive sense, typically referring to a divine or sacrificial love (e.g., John 3:16).[3] In contrast, φιλέω is used in both negative and positive contexts. It can refer to (1) a selfish type of love (e.g., Matt. 23:6), (2) a love of family (e.g., Matt. 10:37), (3) the act of kissing (e.g., Matt. 26:48), and (4) a divine or sacrificial type of love (e.g., John 5:20; 16:27; 1 Cor. 16:22). But just because two near synonyms *can* have different meanings (φιλέω can mean "to kiss," but ἀγαπάω cannot), it does not mean that they *must* have different meanings. As shown above, φιλέω can be used in contexts where one would expect ἀγαπάω. This overlap is also found in the Gospel of John, where the terms are used interchangeably. For example, both terms are used for the Father's love of the Son (3:35; 5:20) and Jesus's love for Lazarus (11:5, 36). Because of this overlap, many NT scholars do not make a distinction between ἀγαπάω and φιλέω in John 21. For instance, D. A. Carson asserts, "I doubt very much that there is an intended distinction."[4]

Second, if we argue for a semantic distinction between ἀγαπάω and φιλέω, then we could also argue for semantic distinctions between other terms in the text where no distinction is intended. As the table shows, this passage contains three other pairs of terms, but it would be very difficult to demonstrate a distinction in meaning.

| First Question and Response | Second Question and Response | Third Question and Response |
|---|---|---|
| ἀγαπᾷς | ἀγαπᾷς | φιλεῖς |
| οἶδας | οἶδας | γινώσκεις |
| βόσκε | ποίμαινε | βόσκε |
| ἀρνία | πρόβατα | πρόβατα |

3. In the Septuagint, the term is found in a negative context (e.g., 2 Sam. 13:15, which refers to Amnon's incestuous rape of his half-sister Tamar), and in the NT it is used of Demas's love for "this present world" (2 Tim. 4:10).

4. Carson, *Exegetical Fallacies*, 51. See also D. A. Carson, *The Gospel according to John* (Grand Rapids: Eerdmans, 1991), 676–77.

When Peter responds, "You *know* that I love You," the first two times οἶδα is used, but on his third reply the verb shifts to γινώσκεις. Should we highlight this shift in our interpretation, or is the shift merely a stylistic variation? Likewise, Jesus restores Peter by telling him, "Feed [βόσκε] My lambs [ἀρνία]," "Shepherd [ποίμαινε] My sheep [πρόβατα]," and "Feed [βόσκε] My sheep [πρόβατα]" (HCSB). Are these variations intended to indicate a different referent or emphasis, or are they merely stylistic? Because we would be hard-pressed to identify any intended distinction between these variations, it makes it unlikely that the difference between ἀγαπάω and φιλέω here is more than stylistic. Most likely these two words (along with the other three sets of words) are used as virtual synonyms.

The focus of the passage is not on the change in terminology but on the number of times Jesus questions Peter. Just as Peter earlier was asked three times if he knew Jesus but denied that he did (John 18:17, 25–27), so Jesus restores Peter by asking him three times regarding his love for his Savior. Or, as F. F. Bruce comments, "What is important is that Peter reaffirms his love for the Lord, and is rehabilitated and recommissioned."[5]

5. F. F. Bruce, *The Gospel of John* (Grand Rapids: Eerdmans, 1983), 405.

# 34

# DISCOURSE ANALYSIS

## Hebrews 1:4–5

### Introduction

It is common knowledge that the chapter and verse divisions are not original but were added later to aid in the reading and studying of the Bible. In the NT, the chapter divisions were made by Stephen Langton (ca. 1150–1228), the archbishop of Canterbury. He added the divisions to the Latin text while he was lecturing at the University of Paris, and subsequent translations and publications came to follow his format. Verse divisions were later added to a Latin and Greek diglot text in 1551 by Robert "Stephanus" Estienne, a printer from Paris. While one certainly ought to be thankful for these helpful divisions (which will probably never be changed), we must also realize that sometimes the divisions were not made at the best locations. Take Hebrews 3–6, for example. One can make a good case that these four chapters should be divided as follows: (1) 3:1–6; (2) 3:7–4:13; (3) 4:14–5:10; (4) 5:11–6:12; (5) 6:13–20. Most likely the best places for the chapter divisions are not where chapters 4, 5, and 6 begin. But how do we determine where a passage begins and ends? This is where discourse analysis has proved to be extremely helpful.

## Overview

Discourse analysis is analyzing a text (or any organized communicative act) with the goal of understanding how it relates to its surrounding context in order to elucidate the author's intended message. It "refers to units of speech longer than a sentence because it usually takes more than a sentence to communicate a complete thought" (Young 247). Or as Moisés Silva observes, "Discourse analysis seeks to understand the ways in which clauses, sentences, and paragraphs are formally related to one another in order to convey meaning."[1] Some of the main features to examine include the following (see Young 251–55, 262–64):

- *Discourse boundaries*: uniformity of content (grammatical, lexical, informational, or teleological), initial marker (orienteers, vocatives, topic statements, or conjunctions), and final markers (doxologies, summaries, or tail-head links).
- *Prominence*: word order, certain words, grammatical features, figures of speech, rhetorical questions, or discourse proportion.
- *Cohesion*: the unity of the various pieces with the whole, flow of thought, and so forth.

## Interpretation

Two key discourse boundaries involve *initial markers* and *final markers*, including the use of *hook words* (catchwords). Guthrie explains the function of hook words: "By use of a common word at the end of one section and at the beginning of the next the author generated a transition between two sections."[2] He continues, "The use of this hook word at the end of one section and the beginning of the next makes a smooth transition between the two."[3]

1. Moisés Silva, *Explorations in Exegetical Method: Galatians as a Test Case* (Grand Rapids: Baker, 1996), 82.

2. George H. Guthrie, *The Structure of Hebrews: A Text-Linguistic Analysis* (New York: Brill, 1994), 96.

3. Guthrie, *Structure of Hebrews*, 96. This concept is similar to "tail-head linkage." Young (254) explains, "A writer may anticipate what will be taken up next as he

The connection between Hebrews 1:4 and 1:5 provides an illustration of this literary feature. In verses 1–4, the author of Hebrews demonstrates how Jesus is superior to the OT prophets. He ends verse 4 with the words "having become as much superior to *angels* as the name he has inherited is more excellent than theirs."[4] He then starts the following section by repeating the theme of angels, which was already mentioned at the end of the previous section: "For to which of the *angels* did God ever say" (1:5). The connection can be illustrated as follows:

> . . . having become as much superior to <u>angels</u> as the name he has inherited is more excellent than theirs. (1:4)
>
> For to which of the <u>angels</u> did God ever say, "You are my Son, today I have begotten you"? Or again, "I will be to him a father, and he shall be to me a son"? (1:5)

Commenting on this literary feature, Ellingworth writes, "Mention of angels acts as a typical 'hook-word' . . . between verses 1–4 and 5–18."[5] Guthrie (*Structure of Hebrews*, 100) maintains that Hebrews 1:4 presents a clear example of a "Hooked Key Word," which refers to a transition being effected by "a characteristic term used in the second unit and introduced in the conclusion of the first unit." Westfall also notes, "There is a cohesive link of ἀγγέλων/ἀγγέλους (angels) in verses 5, 7, and 13 with ἀγγέλων in 1:4."[6]

While most commentators agree that the proper break of the text occurs after verse 4 (even though v. 4 contains the theme of angels found in the subsequent section), not everyone holds this view. For

---

or she closes a section. Thus something will be mentioned at the close of one section and at the start of the next." See also Steven E. Runge, *Discourse Grammar of the Greek New Testament: A Practical Introduction for Teaching and Exegesis* (Peabody, MA: Hendrickson, 2010), 163; Stephen H. Levinsohn, *Discourse Features of New Testament Greek: A Coursebook on the Information Structure of New Testament Greek*, 2nd ed. (Dallas: SIL International, 2000), 197.

4. Emphasis added to this and the next citation.

5. Paul Ellingworth, *The Epistle to the Hebrews*, NIGTC (Grand Rapids: Eerdmans; Carlisle, UK: Paternoster, 1993), 103.

6. Cynthia Long Westfall, *A Discourse Analysis of the Letter to the Hebrews: The Relationship between Form and Meaning*, LNTS 297 (London: T&T Clark, 2005), 92.

example, several commentaries divide the text between verses 3 and 4.[7] But noting the common feature of hook words allows us to break the text at the appropriate location. Thus a pastor who decides to preach through the book of Hebrews will need to decide where best to divide the text. But knowing the best place to make a division is not always easy, and to rely on English versions is not always the wisest course. Consequently, discourse analysis is a helpful tool in determining where to divide a text in order to reveal and preserve the biblical author's communicative structure.

7. R. T. France, "Hebrews," in *The Expositor's Bible Commentary*, ed. Tremper Longman III and David E. Garland, rev. ed. (Grand Rapids: Zondervan, 2006), 13:40; Philip Edgcumbe Hughes, *A Commentary on the Epistle to the Hebrews* (Grand Rapids: Eerdmans, 1977), 50; Arthur W. Pink, *An Exposition of Hebrews* (Grand Rapids: Eerdmans, 1954), 42.

# 35

# DIAGRAMMING

## Hebrews 6:4–6

**Introduction**

Although the core teachings of the Bible are clear, all acknowledge that some passages of the Bible are difficult to interpret. Perhaps one of the most well-known and debated passages in this category is Hebrews 6:4–6. The difficulty of this passage is even evidenced in the way various English versions render this passage.

> For *it is* impossible for those who were once enlightened, and have tasted the heavenly gift, and have become partakers of the Holy Spirit, and have tasted the good word of God and the powers of the age to come, <u>if they fall away</u>, to renew them again to repentance. (NKJV)

> For it is impossible, in the case of those who have once been enlightened, who have tasted the heavenly gift, and have shared in the Holy Spirit, and have tasted the goodness of the word of God and the powers of the age to come, and <u>then have fallen away</u>, to restore them again to repentance. (ESV)

> It is impossible for those who have once been enlightened, who have tasted the heavenly gift, who have shared in the Holy Spirit, who have

tasted the goodness of the word of God and the powers of the coming age and who have fallen away, to be brought back to repentance. (NIV)

Which of the above translations is most faithful to the Greek text? Sentence or phrase diagramming, while not answering all of the issues of this passage, can certainly help to solve some of them.

## Overview

One of the main benefits of diagramming is that it forces the reader to slow down and consider the relationship between various phrases in the text, which then helps elucidate the author's main point.[1] One of the goals in diagramming is for the text to visually represent the syntactical structure of the Greek. The idea is to break the text down into phrases, with the phrases that contain the main proposition(s) to the far left and dependent or subordinate phrases indented further to the right, usually under the word(s) they modify. If a phrase is grammatically parallel to another phrase, it is indented the same distance.

## Interpretation

Using the principles mentioned above, one can create a phrase diagram of Hebrews 6:4–6 (see diagram). Based on the diagram, the main proposition is ἀδύνατον . . . πάλιν ἀνακαινίζειν, "it is impossible . . . to renew again." Typically the main proposition will involve an

---

1. Although there are several types of diagramming, such as line diagramming and arcing, this chapter will focus on phrase diagramming (also sometimes called "sentence-flow" or "thought-flow" diagramming). See Gordon D. Fee, *New Testament Exegesis: A Handbook for Students and Pastors*, rev. ed. (Louisville: Westminster/John Knox, 1993), 65–80; George H. Guthrie and J. Scott Duvall, *Biblical Greek Exegesis: A Graded Approach to Learning Intermediate and Advanced Greek* (Grand Rapids: Zondervan, 1998), 27–53; Douglas S. Huffman, *The Handy Guide to New Testament Greek: Grammar, Syntax, Diagramming* (Grand Rapids: Kregel, 2012), 84–106; KMP 451–58; Benjamin L. Merkle, *Ephesians*, EGGNT (Nashville: B&H, 2016), passim; William D. Mounce, *A Graded Reader of Biblical Greek* (Grand Rapids: Zondervan, 1996), xv–xxiii; Thomas R. Schreiner, *Interpreting the Pauline Epistles*, 2nd ed. (Grand Rapids: Baker Academic, 2011), 69–96.

## CHAPTER 35

Ἀδύνατον γὰρ τοὺς ἅπαξ
φωτισθέντας,
γευσαμένους τε τῆς δωρεᾶς τῆς ἐπουρανίου
καὶ μετόχους γενηθέντας πνεύματος ἁγίου
καὶ καλὸν γευσαμένους θεοῦ ῥῆμα δυνάμεις τε μέλλοντος
αἰῶνος
καὶ παραπεσόντας,
πάλιν ἀνακαινίζειν
εἰς μετάνοιαν,
ἀνασταυροῦντας ἑαυτοῖς τὸν υἱὸν τοῦ θεοῦ καὶ
παραδειγματίζοντας.

indicative or imperative verb,[2] but here the main proposition involves an implied form of the verb εἰμί (is), with the infinitive ἀνακαινίζειν functioning as the subject and ἀδύνατον functioning as the predicate adjective (literally, "to renew again [is] impossible"). Also, notice that the article τούς governs five aorist substantival participles, which are connected with a series of coordinating conjunctions (τοὺς ... φωτισθέντας, γευσαμένους τε ... καὶ ... γενηθέντας ... καὶ ... γευσαμένους ... καὶ παραπεσόντας). For this reason, I placed all five participles (which function as the accusative subjects of the infinitive) under the article to demonstrate that they are parallel. Finally, the prepositional phrase εἰς μετάνοιαν modifies πάλιν ἀνακαινίζειν by expressing purpose or result, and the two present adverbial participles ἀνασταυροῦντας and παραδειγματίζοντας convey the cause or reason why it is impossible for such a person to be renewed again to repentance.

But how does diagramming help solve the interpretive questions that were reflected in the translations above? The first two translations (i.e., the NKJV and the ESV) interpret the last of the five aorist participles (παραπεσόντας) as adverbial, essentially ignoring its parallelism with the first four participles. If παραπεσόντας is adverbial, it could be taken as conditional ("if they fall away," NKJV; so also KJV)

---

2. The main proposition could also involve the two uses of the subjunctive that function as imperatives (i.e., hortatory or prohibitory subjunctives).

or temporal ("then have fallen away," ESV; so also NASB, NRSV). The grammatical construction (five aorist participles governed by the article τούς in 6:4), however, favors reading this participle as substantival (so also CSB). In this case, the author is listing a series of five characteristics of apostates: "those who were once enlightened, who tasted the heavenly gift, [who] became companions with the Holy Spirit, [who] tasted God's good word and the powers of the coming age, and who have fallen away" (HCSB). This interpretation is confirmed by other grammarians, such as Daniel Wallace (633), who writes, "παραπεσόντας is often construed as conditional (a tradition found in the KJV and repeated in most modern translations and by many commentators). But this is unwarranted. . . . If this participle should be taken adverbially, then should we not take the preceding two or three participles the same way? The inconsistency has little basis. Instead, παραπεσόντας should be taken as adjectival, thus making a further and essential qualification of the entire group" (see also Young 156).

Thus, based on the syntactical structure of this passage, it is best to interpret the participle παραπεσόντας not as a hypothetical possibility but as something that indeed has taken place (i.e., one who has fallen away). Some, who were part of the covenant community and displayed genuine evidences of the faith, fell away from the faith and rejected Jesus as the Messiah. It seems to me that the author is using phenomenological language to describe what has taken place. Whether these individuals were truly saved is another question, which this text is not seeking to answer. Rather, the point is that believers should take seriously the warnings of the Bible, since "our God is a consuming fire" (Heb. 12:29). But those who maintain their "confidence firm to the end" (3:14) will enter into God's eternal rest (4:3).

# SCRIPTURE INDEX